My Life Together

My Life Together

L'Arche Communities and the Challenge of Unity

Hilary Wilson

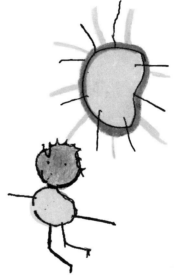

DARTON·LONGMAN+TODD

First published in 2004 by
Darton, Longman and Todd Ltd
1 Spencer Court
140–142 Wandsworth High Street
London SW18 4JJ

ISBN 0–232–52534–X

A catalogue record for this book is available from the British Library.

Designed and produced by Sandie Boccacci
on a G5 PowerMac using QuarkXPress
Set in 10.75/14pt Palatino
Printed and bound in Great Britain by
The Cromwell Press, Trowbridge, Wiltshire

Contents

Foreword

My Life Together has brought back some rich memories of visits to l'Arche during our years in Liverpool. Each visit brought fresh energy and hope to us. One day Grace and I were both feeling exhausted, and then realised that there was still one more commitment in the diary – to spend an evening with l'Arche. It turned out to be reinvigorating. The love that flowed between each member of the community – learning-disabled members and assistants – the respect paid to each in turn over the meal and the quiet space that community prayers brought sent us home renewed in spirit.

Hilary Wilson's book invites us to visit and stay in the world of the different British houses of l'Arche. Stories, songs, poems and pictures give lively flavour. L'Arche is good at celebrating: birthdays are very important. 'A birthday is when we say we're glad you were born' says one learning-disabled member. Yes, for people on the margins it's not obvious that anyone else is glad they were born.

The account of George's illness and death underlined the promise made on inviting someone to make their home with l'Arche – for the rest of their life. He had always had deep fears about dying. Now, his most difficult time was going to hospital for an operation and fearing that he would be left there and not come home. He was never left alone in the months that followed his return. I recall visiting the house soon after his death and hearing of how, when one friend in the community heard that he had died, he wrote him a letter, took it and put it in his hand. I heard too how another had not been allowed to attend her own mother's funeral, because it was assumed she wouldn't understand, but

now went with the whole community to 'a wonderful rousing celebration of joy and sadness'. And one reflection from an assistant
was that George had 'given us incredible gifts in the way he died.
He enabled us all to face our own fears about death and showed
us how to die well.'

George was an 'unlikely giver'. Thérèse Vanier picks up the
phrase in a challenge to us all: 'Unlikely givers, because of an
assumption that those most obviously in need of help have nothing
to give and everything to gain in any caring relationship.' This
book is full of 'unlikely givers', from whom we readers can
receive rich blessings.

Another tale of an 'unlikely giver' moved me very much.
Lizzie describes her cautious approach to Lambeth l'Arche and to
Christian belief. Relationships expressed through banana telephone games at the meal table and quiet sharing at prayer times,
helped her to see a real presence of God in a way she hadn't seen
or experienced in church. When Lizzie was baptised, Primrose, a
learning-disabled member was her godmother, as she regularly
likes to remind her. At the baptism, Primrose signed her with the
sign of the cross in oil on her forehead. As the service ended,
another learning-disabled member, Brian, stepped forward and
gave her 'an immense Brian hug'; again she knew that this was
God, through Brian's strong and unwieldy arms, receiving her
and welcoming her with joy.

The moving account of the footwashing between each member of the community of l'Arche Lambeth on Thursday in Holy
Week tells of people meeting in their weakness, knowing they
need the love and care of the others. L'Arche's emphasis on unity
carries a message for us all – church and beyond. Their search for
unity, Hilary Wilson says, has been very ordinary and very messy,
as all our lives are. Yes, every community needs to learn that
friendships and fellowship are not to be only with people like us.

'Friendships across difference' enrich both parties. One of the themes in the gospels that strikes me regularly is of 'Jesus and the others'. As we have increasingly put away the old, sectarian fears of the others in different churches in Liverpool, we have discovered so many resources and insights that God has stored up for us and that we should have missed if we had stayed tightly confined to Christians like us. And we had much to learn from l'Arche too.

For another l'Arche occasion the three Liverpool ecumenical Presidents, Free Church, Roman Catholic and Anglican, were invited to a gathering of all the l'Arche communities in the country. The final event was in 'the Well' at the West End of the Anglican cathedral. We were presented with three rugs that had been made by the communities – portraying Father, Son and Holy Spirit. For some years from then on, these were hung behind the Presidents' seats at each meeting of our Ecumenical Assembly.

In 'the Well' at the West End of the cathedral, learning-disabled members acted out one of the parables of Jesus, the story of the great supper and those invited who made their excuses. After that, we were all invited to dance in 'the Well'. As we danced, Grace said to me, 'I think heaven must be rather like this!' I repeated that to one of the stalwart lay helpers at the cathedral. He was not so sure that such spontaneity was fitting in the cathedral. 'Yes,' he said. 'But I wouldn't want it to happen too often!'

Hilary Wilson's last chapter is about 'Covenant in Christ'. A friend has taught Grace and I to speak of 'the we of me'. Here Timothy Radcliffe is quoted, challenging our individualism: 'When we can say "We" and flourish humanly, we can understand what it is to say "I am".' The covenant in Christ is mutual – mutual relationships we discover only in letting go of our own terms and conditions.

DAVID SHEPPARD
Wirral 2003

Hilary Wilson with Ian Watkinson, greeting the late Archbishop Derek Worlock and other church leaders on the 'two cathedrals' walk at Pentecost in Liverpool.

Introduction

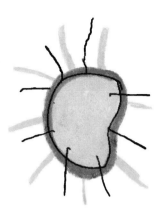

A FEW YEARS AGO Ian Watkinson caught the phrase 'my life together'. We were on the island of Iona for a week, a big group from l'Arche Liverpool, on 'pilgrimage'. Ian struggles with many limitations, including speech; his life has been full of hurts and incomprehension, but many of the people we met on Iona will remember him for his outstretched hand and greeting. Ian is a man of relationship.

This book was conceived as a project to bring together experiences from community life that illustrate the need for and ways towards unity. Unity means healing of divisions and growth in relationships; the reconciliation sorely needed in our broken world and divided churches, as in our homes and families. L'Arche was founded to provide care for people with learning disabilities through faith-based community life. But the issues we face go far beyond the questions of care and disability. These issues include dilemmas that can appear as problems – or as unsought gifts.

One such dilemma arose when the first l'Arche community in Britain opened near Canterbury. Community members belong to different churches, and none. How can we live and pray together, respecting individual allegiances? Amid the opportunities of

1

ecumenism we found ourselves facing the pain of our Christian divisions day by day. Years later, and with more and larger communities, we are still on that rocky road, often frustrated with the blockages and slow progress towards Christian unity. But we know that it is imperative, and part of our purpose as communities.

To help us to cope with these questions, a Pastoral Ecumenical Committee (PEC) was formed, with experienced members of each UK l'Arche community, together with others not from l'Arche who have theological and ecumenical experience. This group continues to meet regularly, and is linked to a small group of church leaders from the different denominations, delegated by their churches to work with l'Arche. Listening to one another in the PEC we realised that we had many experiences, many stories to tell, of the day-to-day incidents in community life that unite us. We know too that people who are vulnerable or powerless, including learning-disabled people, have a particular contribution to make, that risks being unseen, unheard, uncelebrated. So, through the PEC we started to collect some of the stories and experiences of our communities, together with drawings and photographs, poems and songs, all under the heading 'More Unites Us Than Divides Us'.

It takes great effort to write things down; we love retelling the stories – 'remember when ...?' – and looking through the photographs of members past and present, but as in many families, our tradition is mostly oral and easily lost. Several years of persuasion were needed to collect enough material to form a book. Even then the danger was that, put together, it would just be a family album or scrap book, of little interest to non-members. As l'Arche communities we need to reflect regularly on our experience if we are to find meaning and encouragement in the often exhausting daily round of caring and working, cooking and clearing up, falling out and forgiving. So too this collection of everyday life experiences is food for reflection. There is a pattern, first of getting to know one another, building relationships; then loss, facing limitations, even death, before a third phase of deeper, mutual relationships received because of the tough stuff we go through together. The pattern of Relate-Relinquish-Receive forms the core chapters of this book, after the initial chapters introducing l'Arche and the need for unity, and leads to the final chapter on the gift of relationships in Christ.

Most of the stories are not directly about unity. Unity is not something that any of us can 'do'. In the gospel accounts Jesus told his followers to love, to forgive, to be merciful. He did not give a commandment to be united, to be one, but prayed to the Father, just before he died, that his disciples and those who would come after them, would be one (John 17). Unity is gift, received through Jesus' prayer and our prayer, through his death and resurrection and through his relationship in God the Father and the Holy Spirit.

Our experience in l'Arche communities can be no more than a small contribution to the search for healing and unity. But we hope that it will be found relevant, and not just to those who also live in 'intentional' communities, or with learning-disabled people. Human community can be found in families, churches and other faith groups, neighbourhoods, interest groups, places of work and study – everywhere that relationships matter. People who are vulnerable or left out, not only because of disability, suffer most from divisions and so have a particular role in pointing up the need for healing. Their voices need to be heard. We hope that our experience of living together in l'Arche communities can be a source of hope and encouragement to many who struggle and pray for Christian unity, as well as to those committed to peace and reconciliation in the world.

Some of the stories recounted in this book are painful. It is a hard truth that some people who are hurt, disabled or marginalised will never understand the gifts of life that they offer or mediate to others. In order to tell the truth without causing further hurt, some people's names have been changed. However, where full names are used, contributors have given their own agreement for their stories to be shared here.

Many thanks are due to all of the contributors, and to members of the PEC. It is their book. In particular I should like to thank Thérèse Vanier who inspired the theme and collection of material to form a book. There are others too without whom *My Life Together* would not have happened, especially Teresa de Bertodano, Dr Jane Davis of the University of Liverpool, Father Thomas Cullinan, Sister Vreni of Grandchamp, Faye Clerk, Helen Carron, Philippine Sowerby, Revd Graham Cook, Sister Mary Rose Fitzsimmons HHS, and the Ecumenical Scholarship Fund of the Church of England. My deep thanks to all of them and to many other friends who have given encouragement.

HILARY WILSON
L'Arche Liverpool 2003

CHAPTER ONE

What is l'Arche?

> In a divided world, l'Arche wants to be a sign of hope. Its communities, founded on covenant relationships between people of differing intellectual capacity, social origin, religion and culture, seek to be a sign of unity, faithfulness and reconciliation.
>
> *Charter of l'Arche*

I'M A CHILD OF THE SIXTIES, since I was a teenager during those idealistic, optimistic years. In the seventies I discovered terrible poverty, liberation theology and anti-imperialism in Latin America. Then, following personal loss, I met more challenges to faith and commitment through years spent at Taizé, the ecumenical Christian community in Burgundy. I came to live in Liverpool as Margaret Thatcher's first government was elected. All I knew about Liverpool was that in some way the 'issues' of the time were in sharp relief here, that there was a pioneering ecumenical partnership among the churches and their leaders, and that a community of l'Arche had opened. It was some time later that I became part of l'Arche. I knew nothing about 'learning disabilities' (or 'mental handicap' as we said then). I came because

I knew a bit about plants (and the community was starting a horti-culture project) and I wanted to belong among people who were 'poor' and trying to live the Christian gospel in an inner city area of Liverpool. That was still the early eighties; language has changed since then and I hope my idealism has become more mature.

L'Arche itself was born out of the sixties, out of the needs and idealism of that decade. What is now a federation of over one hundred communities, spread throughout the world's continents and cultures, began as just one small household in a French village. The founder, Jean Vanier, was a Canadian academic and his story is well known. Here he tells it himself:

> I was in the Navy for eight years. I left the Navy in 1950 to follow Jesus. Years of searching and of formation began. I lived in a small community in France founded by Father Thomas Philippe, a Dominican priest. It had been founded for lay people who wanted to study philosophy and theology, and to live the gospel values of prayer, poverty and welcome of the poor. I completed a doctorate in philosophy and then started teaching. In 1963, Father Thomas became the chaplain for an institution of thirty men with mental handicaps. He had begun to discover the truth and power of Paul's words, 'but God chose what is foolish in the world to shame the wise; God chose what is weak in the world to shame the strong; God chose what is low and despised in the world, things that are not' (1 Cor. 1:27).
>
> These people who were fragile and vulnerable, whose reason had not developed fully, who had suffered rejection, seemed to be disposed in a special way to receive Jesus' message of love. Their minds were limited, but their hearts were wide open and crying out for love. This seemed to be the realisation of the parable of the wedding feast, to which good, important, capable and religious people are invited, but refuse the invitation

because they are too taken up with their own projects. When the poor, the crippled, the lame and the blind are invited, they come running, with joy! (Luke 14:15–24). Father Thomas suggested that I come and visit his new friends who seemed particularly open and near to Jesus.

To cut a long story short, after meeting Father Thomas' new friends, I stopped teaching philosophy and started to visit different institutions and psychiatric hospitals, where hundreds of people were floundering in pain, rejection, oppression and horrible living conditions. Having lived with the 'winners' in society, I discovered the 'losers'. In 1964 I welcomed from one of these institutions Raphael Simi and Philippe Seux, two men with mental handicaps. They came to live with me in a small, rather broken-down house in Trosly-Breuil, a village in northern France, the same village where Father Thomas was living. This was the beginning of l'Arche.[1]

L'Arche communities are communities with people with learning disabilities and 'assistants' who come to live and work with them. Clearly too, from what Jean Vanier has said above, they are faith-based communities, and the first community with the others that followed it in France is Roman Catholic. However, soon after l'Arche had begun at Trosly-Breuil, there was an initiative in Toronto in Canada, including Anglicans and Christians of other denominations as well as Catholics, and then in India, where interfaith communities were born. Respecting the dignity of each person means respecting their religious identity, which is also a gift each one brings. As Jean Vanier said of these early experiences:

> We welcome people with handicaps, essentially because they have been rejected and seen as worthless, and not because of

their religious affiliation. This has led us to the discovery of our common, broken humanity, and of God's love for each person whatever their origins or religious tradition may be.

The communities of l'Arche are as diverse as the cultures in which they grow up, in North and South America, the Caribbean, Africa, Asia, the Pacific, Australia, Eastern and Western Europe. The challenges faced by l'Arche in the cosmopolitan bustle of Toronto are outwardly very different from the day-to-day getting by that is the reality in the dusty streets surrounding El Arca in Tegucigalpa, Honduras. Even in Northern Europe the history and culture of Poland, along with difficult economic conditions, make life there very different from that in communities across the frontiers in Germany and Holland.

Within the United Kingdom communities reflect our differences from the Scottish Highlands to the South East of England. The first l'Arche community in Britain began in the old Rectory of a small Kent village, not far from Canterbury, the heart of the Anglican communion. Most of the community members with learning disabilities were from Church of England backgrounds, and the assistants were likely to be Roman Catholic; this was our introduction and invitation to ecumenism, with its sensitivities, gifts and pains. The Kent community has grown and now has houses and workshops in Canterbury as well as in two villages.

Ease of visiting wasn't considered too much when the next community began in Inverness in the Highland region of Scotland. Communities are always begun by local groups, so it's not a case of l'Arche 'missionaries' sweeping in and then talking about 'inculturation', but those in Inverness still had to find ways of listening to Presbyterian as well as Catholic and other sensitivities as they prayed and celebrated community life together.

Gather in the Gift of Our Lives

Gather in the gift of our lives,
Blessed, broken, shared.
Reveal our hearts,
to love, like you, to the end.

Abba, Father,
into your hands we place our spirit
and our thirst.

Create in us
a community of people
who welcome weakness,
in covenant with Jesus.
You have given us to each other,
may we stay close enough to hear his heartbeat.

Amen.

Prayer from l'Arche Edinburgh[2]

Two more communities followed, this time in large but very different cities, Liverpool and London, and then a seaside town, Bognor Regis. All these communities began with just one household and in the 25 years or so since have added more homes, usually scattered through a single neighbourhood and often rented from housing associations. In response to the needs for meaningful work and day-time occupations, workshops and horticultural projects have also been established.

Later on there was a Welsh initiative in Brecon and a sister community for Inverness in Edinburgh, followed by l'Arche in Preston, a city with a large multi-ethnic population. Meanwhile three communities had become well established in the Republic of

Ireland, in Kilkenny, Cork and Dublin, and l'Arche has now begun in the North, in Belfast, living across the divisions of that city.

In l'Arche communities people come to live together in very mixed households, three, four or more people with learning disabilities with a similar number of assistants, men and women, all ages from eighteen to eighty years old. Assistants may come from many different countries, with various expectations. Learning to live together is the first essential task, repeated each time assistants come and go (many only stay for a year or two), and as people's needs change, especially with age. This is about unity through difference, not sameness. At first we talked about welcoming people with handicaps or learning disabilities, now many years further on it is clearly they who welcome and receive the assistants who come.

Here Henrieta, Melanie, Isobela and Milan, all in their twenties, describe life in the Coracle in the Liverpool community, where they are assistants. The Coracle is also home to three other assistants and six people with learning disabilities, most of them highly dependent and needing help in everything from dressing and personal care to moving around.

I'm Slovakian; I came here for something new, an adventure. You come because you want to be happy, then you find that you can make other people happy – and that makes you happy.

I'm from Poland. I was here before then when I went home I missed l'Arche, so I came back. It's very challenging; every day you learn something new about yourself and about other people.

I'm from France, and I grew up in l'Arche. I've been in the Coracle before as well and I missed everyone when I was away – I could've stayed with l'Arche in France but I came back here.

10

Our day starts at about 7.00 a.m.; each of us is responsible for helping one person to get up. By 8.30 everyone is downstairs for breakfast together, before Ian, Dave, Nickie and Ying go to the workshop for the day and the social services bus takes Anne and Brian to the training centre. Then for us it's time for housework! Our disagreements are always about housework, not about people; people aren't 'work'. In the afternoon we may have time to rest or to go out, then we're back here by 4.00 p.m., looking out for everyone coming home.

The unlucky one cooks. No, I'd never cooked before; well my mother had showed me a bit, but not for fifteen! I like cooking, but I can get really stressed, trying to have everything ready for six o'clock. Our evening meal is really important; it's the moment in the day when we're all together around the table. I love seeing Nickie so happy, banging the table, and Anne cleaning the last pea from her plate, and Ian talking. There's always something happening, and we've got more energy when we're together.

Washing up together is often funny, then we gather in the living room for prayers. It's a quiet time, a good time. We light a candle in the middle and turn the lights out. Someone reads a short bit from the Bible, or perhaps a poem; we listen and are silent together, then anyone can share any prayers out loud. Brian starts the 'Our Father' and we sing a simple song. After that we stay together, just chatting, or maybe someone plays the guitar or puts some music on – until it's about 9.30 and time to help each person to bed.

Ying is a challenging woman; she can be really happy or really angry. Sometimes her eyes that can't see at all are completely shining with joy. She changes my mood too.

11

Nickie can't speak with her mouth, or stand by herself, but her eyes tell you how much she loves you or if she's sad or she wants to get up and walk. She has a big, big heart. She is forgiving and open to everyone.

Milan, from the Czech Republic, describes David:
Dave's very calm. You need to take your time and relax. He's very sensitive and loves being out in the open air, on the beach or in the country. It's a big challenge here; often at the end of the day I sit down and think what's happened and why . . . it's a good way to get to know myself and other people, and to try to understand . . . well I just pray then.

Just as no two families are the same, every l'Arche household is distinctive, but houses and communities have many elements and an ethos in common. Maggie Smith has been an assistant in the Kent community for many years, and reflects on a day there:

To become an assistant at l'Arche is to enter a very ordinary reality of home, work and community. A life full of all the usual round: a friend's birthday, going to the cinema, visiting friends, going shopping, going to church and to each other's churches. And yet it is a reality that is quite transformed. I wait for the minibus taking me into work and as it draws up Alec, Pete and Yvonne greet me with such warmth you wouldn't think it was only yesterday we saw each other. As we get out Alec shouts after me every morning 'Don't work too hard!' Sometimes each morning can feel like a celebration of the sheer fact of being alive and on this earth together.
    Work is more serious (contrary to Alec's injunction). We sell what we make on its own worth, not as an object of another's charity. It is very important for someone used to

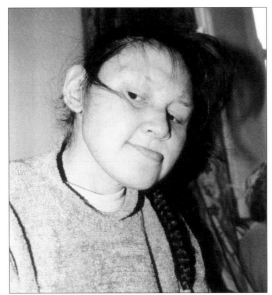

Ying Cheung

David Swan

13

being put aside to see that what they make has value; people pay money to buy it. Back home we share the cooking. Supper, the important meal of the day, is not just a time to eat, but a time to relax together, to catch up on each other's day. 'To love someone is to waste time with them' says Jean Vanier. It is so important to 'waste' time, simply to enjoy the gift of the person. After supper, for those who wish there is prayer. Peter at his birthday party gave thanks for each person in the room. It's not something we say much in the day-to-day conversation, but in this gentle and tender space people speak to God what is deepest in their hearts and you hear the great love there is within each person.

Workshop life is an important part of many of our communities. Two decades ago there was little statutory 'daytime provision' for people with learning disabilities who were not expected to contribute or even to do very much at all. L'Arche workshops began with an emphasis on learning practical skills and producing saleable goods – candles, greeting cards, rugs, potted plants, garden furniture and ornaments. Products are chosen because they can be seen in use and look beautiful, enabling the producer to see the link between other people's needs and his or her own contribution and value. Now with changing needs, and more work opportunities for people with learning disabilities in 'mainstream' employment, l'Arche community workshops have diversified to include other therapeutic elements and 'retirement' activities for older members. Workshops also employ learning-disabled people who live outside l'Arche communities, such as Ian Ross who illustrated his first day in the workshop at l'Arche Inverness (see opposite).

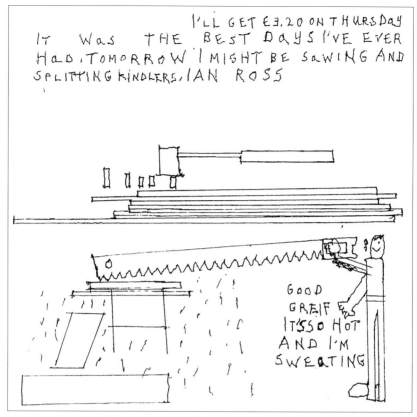

First Day in the Workshop by Ian Ross

The assistants in the Coracle in Liverpool spoke just now of their wonder as they got to know David, Nickie and Ying. Peter's birthday was a source of wonder too. Of course it's not that easy all the time. There is a great deal of pain, loss and sheer confusion in the lives of many people with learning disabilities, and in different ways and to different extents in the lives of us, the assistants. Community life brings all of this out, hence the challenge that Milan and the others spoke about and struggle with.

Those with mental handicaps possess the pains of the heart as well as the gifts of the heart. They present a challenge as well as a gift to those of us who live at the level of the intellect and can so easily conceal our real needs from others and even from ourselves. Their gift is to reveal the true humanity that we share: the same deep need to be loved and to love, to belong and to be valued for who we are, to choose, to have the opportunity to develop our full potential, and to reach out and touch the spiritual.[3]

Thérèse Vanier founded the Kent community of l'Arche and is a medical doctor and elder sister of Jean Vanier. Her words here are tough.

The gift of revealing 'the true humanity that we share' is indeed a gift, one from perhaps unlikely givers.

'Unlikely givers' because of an assumption that those most obviously in need of help have nothing to give and everything to gain in any caring relationship. Those who do the caring know differently and increasingly say so. One can see this in the hospice movement, people who are dying and their families are cared for and re-empowered; among patients who suffer from AIDS and those working alongside them; among people who are homeless and those who seek to help them recover not only a roof over their heads but a sense of their own dignity and value.

It seems that one of the most precious gifts offered by these unlikely givers is that they are calling people to unity. So often they carry within themselves a sense of being fragmented, lost, unrecognised. And here one could include many young people today who feel lost in the face of the dismemberment of values in our world, to the extent of losing any sense of good and bad. They are often tolerant and generous and the broadening of their perceptions has a positive value but it also leads to confusion and a state of inner fragmentation.

All these people and others besides, call out for unity among those who care for them, for unity in the world that surrounds them; and this includes the fragmented Church of Christ and the brokenness that lies at the heart of the religious dimension of humanity.

International Council of l'Arche [4]

This gift, this connectedness with the shattered world that we live in, answers some of the 'what are we here for questions?' that we must ask if we are to continue. We come to many commitments, l'Arche among them, seeking to be happy, seeking to belong. We hit walls, mostly made of our own limitations, and our initial ideals seem inadequate. To return to my own story, when I went to Latin America straight after university my hopes and expectations were turned upside down, not just by the poverty of the people I met, but by the capacity for life and the hope they shared. Among the people I was with in those countries there was a struggle for justice and for better opportunities. This is true too, up to a point, of life with people with learning disabilities. But only up to a point. Disability itself does not go away, even if we can struggle for opportunities, dignity, justice. What I discovered in Latin America and in l'Arche, even if I couldn't put words on it, was that I needed to find life with 'poor' people who already had value, unique gifts to offer. The hope, mysteriously, lies in - actively waiting on God together.

If l'Arche has continued and grown and if some of us have stayed and grown in community life, it is because of this gift, this mystery. The mystery that people who are less articulate and often rejected can turn over generally accepted values, revealing the true humanity that we share, crying out for wholeness and justice in the world around them. The following chapters will explore and celebrate through first-hand stories the experiences that have called some people to enter more deeply into that shared humanity, expressed in this prayer, said, sung and signed (in Makaton, an adapted form of British Sign Language) in l'Arche communities throughout Britain:

L'Arche Prayer in the UK

Father, through Jesus, our Lord and our Brother
we ask you to bless us.
Grant that l'Arche be a true home
where the poor in spirit may find life,
where those who suffer may find hope.
Keep in your loving care all those who come.

Spirit of God, give us greatness of heart
that we may welcome all those you send.
Make us compassionate, that we may heal and bring
    peace.
Help us to see, to serve and to love.

O Lord, through the hands of your little ones, bless us,
through the eyes of those who are rejected, smile on us.

O Lord, grant freedom, fellowship and unity to all your children
and welcome everyone into your Kingdom.

Amen.

CHAPTER TWO

Why Unity?

All these people and others besides, call out for
unity among those who care for them, for unity in
the world that surrounds them; and this includes the
fragmented Church of Christ and the brokenness that lies at
the heart of the religious dimension of humanity.

International Council of l'Arche

THE VIOLENCE ON 11 September 2001 overshadowed all our
lives and all other events at that time. One of the stories abruptly
pushed off the front pages of the newspapers was the tragedy
being played out around the Holy Cross Primary School in the
Ardoyne area of Belfast. Every morning and afternoon children
ran the gauntlet of jeering adult protesters. Several years on from
the signing of the Good Friday peace accord the disunity still goes
deep. Those of us living outside the Province have had to learn
that the signing of a peace accord and its implementation are two
very different things, and we have felt the hurt of what goes on
around that Belfast estate in a rather uncomprehending way.
What we do understand is that young children are being
damaged, another generation is being scarred. The divisions and
violence are shocking because the victims are vulnerable children.

We may not understand the attitudes of the adults on either side of the argument but the lives, faces and futures of the children call out for unity, for listening, forgiveness and the long slow rebuilding of relationships.

Yvonne Klein Bentley was born with cerebral palsy. At times during her life she has known exclusion, expressed in this poem:

Lessons

Childhood should be a time
when you are too young to learn
that 'friends' can be bought
with chocolate and sweets
and the loan of a toy;

that the playmates you've got
disappear, when someone else
comes to the door, and then
once again you're alone,
on your own.

When 'enemies' call truce
so that they can agree
to torment you;
and they leave you at one door
to sneak out the other,

and there's no one who knows,
for you're 'not to tell tales'
and this state is normal –
and will go on for ever . . .

In my teens my hurt was too deep,
and pride reinforced

the lessons I'd learnt,
so I scorned to reach out
to their olive branch offered.

It's taken long years
and hard work to unlearn
the lessons I'd learnt.

Vulnerable people, whether they are children in Belfast or in Baghdad, refugees in Afghanistan, people with mental illness or with severe disabilities, call out for unity in the world that surrounds them because disunity damages their lives, as it damages us all. This is the experience of young children in fraught family situations too. People who are excluded call for inclusion, for a proper recognition of their humanity.

In the last chapter, assistants in l'Arche Liverpool and Maggie Smith from the Kent community talked about the importance of mealtimes together. People with learning disabilities come to l'Arche communities in a number of ways. In Britain this often involves social services and the local health authority. Some years ago when the old 'long stay' mental handicap hospitals were closing I visited a young woman to whom we hoped to offer a place in l'Arche. The staff on the ward where Dot was living were hospitable and invited me to join them for their morning break so I sat down at the table with them for coffee and toast. Dot cannot walk unaided and cannot speak, but does like coffee, the smell of toast and the company of other people, so she shuffled over on her bottom and looked up at the table pleadingly. There was no place for her, nor for the dozen other disabled patients in the ward. I looked down at Dot and realised what it meant to be excluded, to have no place at table.

Who I Am

This is my home and my roots.
These are the people who've held me.
These are my fears, times of hurt goodbye.

And you will know me and love me;
I will enfold you in who you are
I will lead you to the lowly
And you will cry to me and know who I am.

These are my friends I've received.
These are the hopes I will live.
And these goodbyes I have prayed to you.

I am the way you will live.
I am the truth you receive.
Share in my death with the hope of life.

l'Arche Edinburgh

Belonging is essential to being, to knowing one's own identity. In East Africa the Kikuyu people sing at the initiation ceremony for a newborn child: 'We are because I am; I am because we are.' The South African word 'ubuntu' translates roughly 'I belong, therefore I am'. Despite our Western cult of individualism and movement away from such communality, we still experience unity through belonging, through family, school, sport or other club activities. Following the fortunes of big football clubs increasingly fills the 'I belong, therefore I am' need in many lives. Belonging needs to be expressed and celebrated with rituals and symbols. At many funerals in Liverpool the coffin is decorated with flowers in team colours, headstones in Merseyside cemeteries often carry football insignia and one of the problems of trying to move a stadium is what to do with the turf on which the ashes of so many deceased followers have been scattered. Players and supporters do need one another, though the relationship between them has limits. Only the chosen few get to play on the pitch and this sort of belonging divides as it unites. Loyalty excludes rival teams.

In the days following the Hillsborough disaster, when nearly 100 Liverpool supporters died as barriers collapsed at a Sheffield ground, I was very moved by the sense of unity and solidarity on the streets of Liverpool that transcended all Liverpool–Everton team rivalry. As human beings we yearn for communion, for *koinonia*, a relationship of mutual belonging, empathy, acceptance, 'growing-in-the-right-place', ultimately 'growing into God'. This sort of belonging is not about skill or fitness. It is about a mutual recognition of gifts, but gifts within our weaknesses, our limitations. Christian faith both reveals and expresses our belonging, and calls us to the deeper and ultimate communion.

Susan Jones writes:

George Munnerley joined l'Arche Liverpool in 1977, less than a year after the community opened. He had previously lived with his father who'd cared for him until his own death. George was well known locally; for many years he'd pushed a hand cart around, selling firewood and cleaning supplies. He had spent much of his time on the streets, begging for money and food, stealing biscuits from local supermarkets, giving sweets to children and sadly also finding himself the butt of ragging and taunts. When he came to l'Arche George had few social habits; he hated washing or changing his clothes and ate food that had been thrown out. He was distressed after the death of his father and if anything his disturbance deepened during those first years in the community. George appeared tormented, endlessly questioning where his money was, what he would eat, what would happen next . . . he was never heard to say yes to anything.

In the seven years or so that he lived in the community before he died, George journeyed from constantly saying 'I'm no good am I?' to a rather contented refrain of 'Well that's alright isn't it?' Susan continues:

Slowly things began to change – George became more peaceful and was gradually re-introduced to the group at the meal table. In a daily log that was kept it was recorded one day: 'George smiled today.' That became a more regular occurrence as he discovered a life without constant anxiety and torment. George began to laugh; long, deep belly laughs which were infectious to all around him. He ate most things and even

George Munnerley

developed a liking for new clothes. He put on weight, so much so that the portly, bearded, laughing George of the last years of his life bore little resemblance to the emaciated, tormented and miserable figure of his earlier years.

Thérèse Vanier takes up the story:

> What could the community offer George? Not some impressive programme; just the simple but difficult thing of living with him, seeking what help was available, praying . . . for in George was fear, violence, apathy and above all a sense of being powerless, of no value. In other words all that we find around us in our world. By little steps the household which welcomed George found small ways, during meals, on holiday, in the workshop and in household jobs, of valuing him.

We shall return to George's story in a later chapter. George journeyed from rejection to acceptance, to being-through-belonging. But belonging in itself is not communion, does not necessarily lead us to wider or deeper unity, just as the sense of belonging that some football supporters take with them to the grave brings them no nearer the rival team. Going back to the children of Holy Cross School in Belfast, the unity that their lives call for must go beyond being secure in one's own group. What we seek in a divided world is communion across humanity, a wider sense of common belonging that can lead us to find healing of the divisions that kill, oppress, exclude. What else do vulnerable people bring to this search? In other words how do vulnerable people unite *other* people? The experience of living with George through his slow, painful journey did unite the community around him, though always at a price. This 'price' is in a sense the theme of the rest of this book and is very real – some families are put under intolerable pressure when there is a severely disabled child to be cared for for years on end.

The Holy Things of God

The holy things of God are here,
Blest and broken, quenching fear;
God's holy people, gather near,
Made one with tears of love.

If we but knew the gift he brings,
How he longs to gather in,
And share with us the living spring
Cascading to our hearts.

In Christ there is no east or west,
One the host, and one the guests
Whom Jesus kneads with holiness;
Made one in heart and love.

l'Arche Edinburgh

Henri Nouwen's life was a long struggle for peace and acceptance, from which many people have benefited as they read his books. He spent the last ten years of his life at l'Arche Daybreak in Toronto, Canada. There Henri became Adam's assistant and the experience touched him deeply. Here Henri describes how Adam became a source of unity to those around him:

Adam in his total vulnerability calls us together around him. The weakest members in our midst are, in fact, the assistants. We come from different countries and our commitments are ambiguous at best. Some stay longer than others, but most move on after one or two years. Closer to the centre of our community life are Raymond, Bill, John, and Trevor, who are relatively independent but cannot make it all on their own and still need much help and attention. They are permanent members of the family. They are with us for life and they keep calling us to be present to them. They call us to be honest. Because of them and of their weakness we must find unity among us, so conflicts never last very long, tensions are talked out, and disagreements resolved. And right in the heart of our community are Rose and Adam, both deeply handicapped and needy, and the weaker of the two is Adam.

Adam is the weakest of us all, but without any doubt the strongest bond between us all. Because of Adam there is always someone home; because of Adam there is a quiet rhythm in the house; because of Adam there are moments of silence and quiet; because of Adam there are always words of affection, gentleness, and tenderness; because of Adam there is patience and endurance; because of Adam there are smiles and tears visible to all; because of Adam there is always space for mutual forgiveness and healing . . . yes, because of Adam there is peace among us. How otherwise could people from such different nationalities and cultures, people with such an odd variety of handicaps, whether mental or not, live together in peace?

Adam truly calls us together around him and moulds this motley group of strangers into a family. Adam is our true peacemaker. How mysterious are the ways of God: 'God chose those who by human standards are weak in order to shame the strong, those who by human standards are common and contemptible – indeed who count for nothing – to reduce to nothing all those who do count for something, so that no human being might feel boastful before God' (1 Cor. 1:27–30). Adam gives flesh to these words of Paul. He teaches me the true mystery of community.[5]

If vulnerable people call for unity among those around them, it is clear from Henri Nouwen's experience that we have to respond in some way if we are to receive the gift of unity. Opportunities pass us by each day, often unnoticed. One evening in a community house in l'Arche Lambeth provided such a moment – Christine Adams was able to notice, respond and receive:

> Christine, and her husband Tony, the local Methodist Minister, were having supper in a community household. Afterwards, while people were washing up, Laurence, who has a severe mental handicap and does not speak, became bored and fractious. He took a guitar and began strumming in a noisy, tuneless way. After a moment Christine began to pick out a tune on another guitar. Through their combined offering there was music, and when they finished there was a round of applause. A smile spread from one side of Laurence's face to the other. Tony said that he saw, for the first time, what it meant to 'grin from ear to ear'. They began playing again and others joined in with percussion instruments and humming.[6]

Each one of us is gifted, because we are created bearing God's image, an infinite variety of the different facets of the nature of God, each person unique. But we need one another if those gifts are to be revealed. Gifts are revealed through relationship. Laurence was not born to be a virtuoso guitar player; that evening Christine and Laurence revealed one another's gifts and drew others together around them. We come to know our gifts by the way we are treated; in relationship the gift that has been hidden is revealed. Relationship also reveals the limitations of each of us and, if we allow it, can lead us to greater honesty and openness with ourselves and one another, and greater inter-dependence. And so we grow, each more fully human, more fully people of communion, more fully realising the image of God that we bear.

Joy

What feeling I have in my heart,
a warm feeling.
No-one can take away joy
because it is alive in my heart.

Like in church, you have a happiness,
not a deadness.
God says happiness is good.
We're all the same;
we're all one,
not two people.
Like time – a clock goes the whole way round.
Within myself, I'm one.
Joy keeps you warm.

James Fraser, l'Arche Inverness

What a gift to feel that happiness, that warmth, that oneness, and in church too, and to know it as a gift from God! Lack of oneness in and among churches is painful and for people with learning disabilities and for many others who have more experience of community life and prayer than of church history and doctrine, Christian disunity is especially confusing and contradictory. Church history and doctrine are important but a lack of unity affects us all deeply. Just as the faces of the children of Holy Cross Primary School in Belfast strike us with the scandal and sheer wrongness of the sectarian divisions around them so the hurt and confusion felt by other vulnerable people point up the scandal and damage of all Christian disunity.

L'Arche is discovering the call to ecumenism at many levels –
locally, nationally and internationally. Shortly after the attacks in
the USA on 11 September 2001, the three international church
representatives for l'Arche wrote:

> We would affirm the importance of the communion that you
> share. It encourages communion to grow among all Christians.
> Each of us is called to remain faithful to the richness of our
> own tradition and to be enriched by those of others. Your
> communities are places of unity because the vulnerable are at
> the centre, because they are recognised as a sign of the
> presence of Jesus, and so as a source of unity. Wasn't it in the
> poverty of the cross and by the gifts of his life that Jesus brought
> together in unity all the children of God dispersed throughout
> the world?
>
> As you know, all churches are called to grow in unity, not
> in order that Christians might become stronger and more
> numerous, but so that the world might believe that God sent
> his Son to save it (John 17). Unity among Christians is essential
> for the world that is in need of mutual affection, love and
> peace. God does not want to unite only the churches, but all
> of humanity. By living together in love, with all of your religious
> and cultural diversity, you show that the unity that God desires
> is possible and is a source of happiness for all.
>
> *Bishop Roger Herft, Australia, Anglican*
> *Revd Jim Cowie, Scotland, World Council of Churches*
> *Bishop Gérard Daucourt, France, Roman Catholic*

> For in him all the fullness of God was pleased to dwell, and
> through him to reconcile to himself all things, whether in earth
> or in heaven, making peace by his death on the cross.
>
> *Col. 1:19–20*

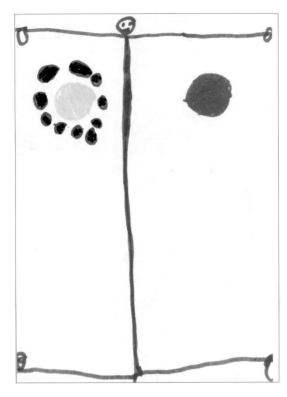

'Our Faith Group was considering the theme of peace and each of us drew a picture to illustrate this. Nick drew this picture and explained "Jesus died to bring us peace ... and, yes that's the sun and the moon and the stars ...".'
Nick Ellerker, *Peace*

Ecumenical communities experience both church unity and disunity in daily life. In l'Arche, as in other 'mixed' communities and in many families, we live, pray, eat, work, rest and celebrate (and agree and disagree) together every day. We then go our separate ways on Sunday mornings, to the various places of worship of the different traditions we all belong to. Choice and diversity are good things and Christian unity does not mean Christian sameness, but there are moments when the crunch comes and difference means division, contradiction and incomprehension. Father Kevin Kelly, a Roman Catholic moral theologian, spoke of the difficulty Christians can have when 'they fail to make experience-sense of their faith and faith-sense of their experience'.

Living and worshipping in the denominations that different community members belong to means that we cannot usually receive holy communion together without transgressing the norms or teaching of certain churches, norms which if taken all together actually contradict one another. This is felt as we attend one another's churches and especially at those moments when the Eucharist is celebrated within a l'Arche community. Sacrament of unity – and yet of disunity, so long as our churches remain separated.

> Susan was confirmed as a member of the Church of England several years ago, with a number of other learning-disabled members of the community. Family and friends were present as the Bishop of Dover asked simply, 'Do you want to walk with Jesus?' Since then Susan has been able to receive communion at Anglican community Eucharists, and it was explained to her that she could receive a blessing at the Roman Catholic Eucharists. More recently Susan has stopped receiving, pointing to her head for a blessing when she approaches the priest. Susan no longer receives communion at any community Eucharists, when we gather together to celebrate and offer our common life to God and to each other.
>
> *l'Arche Kent*

As fellow members of a 'body' of faith members, there are times when we carry one another in faith. There are moments too when we feel the pain in the broken body of Christ and then need to grow through our own hurt and anger. Pain alerts us to the body's needs and can lead us to seek healing. Perhaps Susan's spontaneous change was her protest, conscious or not, coming from her confusion and the contradiction she faced. Just as divisions, conflicts and exclusion of one another diminish humanity as a whole and the dignity of being human, Christian disunity is scandalous because it breaks up the body we are called to belong to. The broken body of Christ is mystical reality and it is felt reality for many who cannot understand, but who live in communion at a profound level.

> Bella had spent virtually her entire life, almost 40 years, in long-stay hospitals before she came to l'Arche, bringing her great anxieties and immense neediness. Somewhat to our surprise, church (where she is a confirmed member), community prayers and liturgies were immediately places of reverence and communion for her. When she realised that at some community Eucharists she was excluded from receiving holy communion, she felt fury and inconsolable sadness. Eventually, at the end after others had left, she would go to the priest, though she had no words. He told her he was sorry. She forgave him warmly and they lived the communion of a hug. She was consoled. Only to experience the same incomprehensible rejection next time. Now, as she stares hungrily at the paten, she often pleads with the priest as he attempts to give her a blessing 'Little bit, just a little bit!' Often I have myself felt unable to receive communion at the Eucharist because it seemed such a travesty of Jesus' own action, breaking the bread of life and saying 'Take this all of you' (all, even those who deny and betray and run away). Beyond her personal pain, I felt the scandal that we had educated Bella into church divisions of which she had no notion before and which she will never, never understand.
>
> *Chris Sadler, l'Arche Lambeth*

These experiences do not call for a brushing over of differences and the very significant issues that divide us. Rather they are like litmus paper that signals what is there, in this case issues that we can get used to, accommodate ourselves to, abdicate responsibility for. Vulnerable people are telling us something different, something urgent, about our divided reality and the need to move to heal it.

It is too easy to get stuck on the questions of whether we can receive holy communion with one another. Assistants in a group in a l'Arche community were complaining with great feeling one day about the impossibility and injustice of 'church rules' when retired Anglican Bishop Stephen Verney exclaimed even more passionately that we were 'called beyond the Eucharist, *to do the thing itself!'* In other words to put the meaning of the Eucharist into practice in our lives, our relationships, our communities. To live beyond the differences, even though they remain real or to recognise that, using the slightly clichéd expression, 'more unites us than divides us'. Another priest friend of l'Arche put it more theologically:

> 'Belonging' relationships, and the reality of unity are there before we realise them. Unity is both an existing reality and an aspiration, what is yet to be. We can see this in all sorts of groups and in families. The urgency of ecumenism is not just a longing for corporate union in faith and life, but is because not being in union is a counter sign of the mystery of Christ and the reality of God.

What are the steps to this 'corporate union in faith and life'? There are many ways to unity and reconciliation, to building what in l'Arche we call 'covenant relationships' – relationships that we receive and grow into, relationships that go beyond differences into deeper ways of belonging. Unity is not just a question of being nicer to one another. There are good times to be had learning to 'relate' together but there are also times of letting go, losses to face. And then new life. An Anglican contemplative nun recently described the three R's of prayer as 'Relax, Relinquish, Receive'. I want to hijack and modify her three R's as the three R's of a way to unity: RELATE, RELINQUISH, RECEIVE. These three R's will form the basis of the following chapters as we look at the ways that our lived experience in l'Arche draws us towards deeper unity.

The following dedication was read by the Northern Europe communities of l'Arche to church leaders of different denominations at a celebration in Liverpool's Anglican Cathedral.

> We live in a divided world.
> We belong to a divided church.
> What we see in the world about us, we live in our hearts.
> What the world lives, we live.
> What the church lives, we live.
>
> In our society, we are surrounded by a culture of division,
> which feeds on division and seems to thrive on division.
> Yet we know that we cannot continue in divisions that threaten
> to destroy our world. Even though the church has not been
> protected from the forces of division, we see the church as our
> hope.
>
> We seek unity.
> We thirst for unity.
> We are here with you today because our hearts yearn for unity.
>
> As we live with each other in our communities,
> we learn more and more how division begins in our hearts.
> We are a broken people in a broken world.
> We are all poor; we are all weak.
> We know our need of one another.
> We know our need of God.
> And we are all invited to the feast in the Kingdom.

CHAPTER THREE

Relate

When you walk through the storm, hold your head up high,
and don't be afraid of the dark . . .
Walk on through the wind, walk on through the rain
though your dreams be tossed and blown;
walk on, walk on with hope in your heart,
and you'll never walk alone, you'll never walk alone!

Richard Rodgers and Oscar Hammerstein II

'You'll never walk alone!' – just a football song? Maybe, but for lots of people those words have tremendous power; they always make me think of a friend who really does hold her head up high when her team has won. My friend is a gifted artist and dancer as well as a keen football supporter and she has learning disabilities. Her disability proved too difficult for her parents and she has suffered greatly through having no contact with her immediate family since she was four years old. She still dreads Christmas each year because of its 'family' associations. But during our community pilgrimages this same friend is always walking up in the front, her head as high as when her team wins.

Christmas, friendship, games, journeying together: all are

images of being together, building relationships, getting to know one another, celebrating life. They are vital elements of family life and certainly have a big part to play in l'Arche communities, in discovering and making real our human oneness. There's also much that is very ordinary. Bernard Potts described his first impressions of community life in l'Arche Preston as 'doing the dishes, answering the telephone, mowing the lawn and thinking up gripping new ways to serve pasta'. But he talked too about building relationships: 'The words between us are repetitive, and usually have a limited meaning, but that doesn't matter. They are like a ball that we throw to one another. The ball itself isn't important, it just helps us to relate to each other, to share an experience.'

James Fraser, a poet from Inverness previously quoted, expresses 'You'll never walk alone' in terms of his faith, in his poem:

The Moon and the Stars
I always say that when I see
the stars, the moon and the sun,
He's here, God's here,
and you can't always see Him
but He's there all the time.
You feel Him, it's touched,
it's a goodness in God, a goodness in yourself,
a goodness in the world.

Do not be afraid of the dark . . . God's there!
I still have faith.
Faith is healing and God is healing,
and He's there all the time.
And the angels are with you.

James says 'Faith is healing and God is healing'. In our welcome of one another it's not just our relationships that are healed but also ourselves. None of us comes to community life whole or in one piece, whether we have learning disabilities or not. Ruth Goodheir had been an assistant in l'Arche Inverness, and after several years away, returned and was welcomed back into the community. She describes her experience:

> I was delighted to find that the room I was given had a table large enough for drawing and painting in my rest times. During my first few weeks I began a drawing of a little girl making mud pies, but she was at the edge of a volcanic crater. She was like a wee Glasgow street urchin, just the kind of wee girl I once was. In the distance, walking towards her was an adult woman, bent almost double under a huge burden. As I worked on this picture I felt God saying to me 'Come and play. Come and play with me at the very beginning of creation. It's all right to become a child again.' The adult woman is also me, my adult self, worried, guilt-ridden, burdened.
>
> As I shared the daily life of the community, making cakes with Barbara, painting eggs with Corinne, singing with Derek, planting seeds with Stephen, making candles with Susan, I felt I was becoming this little child again, playing in the mud. God wanted me to leave my adult, burdened self for a while.
>
> I'm not saying something sweet and sentimental here; far from it. The mud is volcanic, full of pain and anger and rawness. There's a lot of suffering here in the community and also in myself. But God was telling me it's possible to handle this mud *lightly* – to play, to sing, to take my part in the great creative act of life.
>
> As we move towards the season of Advent and the mystery of the Incarnation, I pray that I can keep alive in my

Ruth Goodheir, *Girl with mud pies*

heart the little child playing in the mud, so that I can be ready to welcome the child Jesus.

We are welcomed by one another, hurts and all, and before Christmas, through the weeks of Advent, we prepare to welcome the Christ child, though some have mixed feelings. Ivan McCullagh and Mark Mitchell, also from L'Arche Inverness, discussed Advent:

'What does Advent mean?'

'It's about putting names in a hat.'

'What happens then?'

'We have a prayer for Advent.'

'Why?'

'Because it's about Jesus. It's about waiting for God's birthday.'

'What happens to the names in the hat?'

'We take a name out . . .'

'And then we give them a surprise?'

'It's a secret.'

'We each get the name of an advent-friend or Christ-kin, who we're nice to and do special things for during Advent. We keep their name a secret until Christmas when we give them a present.'

'What else do we do?'

'We light the candles on the wreath and have a Christmas tree and put the decorations on the tree. Getting ready to celebrate Jesus.'

Advent can be a wonderful time of year, preparing for Christmas and bringing together hopes and memories, and all sorts of customs from different countries. Some of these customs, baking and sharing cakes and biscuits, candles and lights, the Advent wreath, offer plenty to do, see, touch and eat. But this is not just tradition and nostalgia. In l'Arche communities we often emphasise how the visual is more important than the verbal in our celebrations and liturgies but we can all be people of the heart, whether or not we have learning disabilities, and the mysteries of faith certainly need to be received at heart as well as at head level. As Ruth said of her own experience, we can all learn 'to play, to sing, to take part in the great creative act of life'.

Love
Time doesn't stop.
Love is invisible.
The product of love is an invisible hand.
God is love.
It's important to love other people.
They are warm.
Making cakes and washing dishes is love.

The saucer and the candle help each other.
The candle gives light, the saucer is round.
You need both.
Love must have another word for it.

James Fraser

A central part of our Christmas celebrations in l'Arche communities is 'The Play' when we gather to act out the story of Christ's birth. No two plays have ever been the same and there are always unscripted moments, such as the time when 'Mary', played on this occasion by a woman who could become very distressed, dumped the 'Christ-child' doll in the straw in the middle of a carol, and disappeared from the scene yelling 'Toilet!'. Somehow 'The Play' is prayerful and makes us laugh. This celebration of the incarnation is incarnation itself. For a learning-disabled woman in the community, coming to terms with her own childlessness, being Mary is a solemn moment, a realisation.

Thérèse Vanier tells of the play one Christmas Eve in l'Arche Lambeth:

The story of Bethlehem was evoked through the memories of the local townsfolk. A team of 'investigative journalists' descended on Bethlehem several years after the event, and were cross-questioning people about the strange happenings. John was cast as a townsman. Now John is a man who has a constant struggle to find any hope in reality. He was asked: 'Well what was the name of this child?' 'Jesus', said John. 'Never heard of him', said the journalist. 'You will', said John, 'You will . . .' I still do not know if that was in the script or if it leapt from John's hurt heart.

Philip Yates, a learning-disabled member of l'Arche Lambeth, once said that 'a birthday is when we say we're glad you were born'. For many people on the margins for whatever reason it's not obvious that anyone else is glad they were born. Birthday celebrations are important, to celebrate the uniqueness, the gift of each person, so they take a bit of thought and creativity. Much of the fun of a birthday party depends on how much the person celebrated is in the know. For some it must all be a surprise – the food, the decor, the cake, guests, gifts . . . while for others it's the day when 'I can choose *everything*'. Most of us want some element of choosing, laced with the joy of surprises. Either way it's about letting ourselves be loved.

Patrick is a desperately anxious, insecure man who will never have any idea, at least in this life, of the great number of people he touches with his friendship. (I hope that that will be one of many things that he'll find out in heaven.) So his birthday party needs to be a delicate mix of security ('yes it will happen, on this day, and so-and-so will be there, and we will have sausages and gravy and mash') and loving surprises – a special friend coming, a new football shirt in the right colours, the table and the birthday cake ingeniously decorated in a personal and fun theme.

With Patrick the question is whether he can bear to sit with a group for long enough to receive all that each person wants to give and to say. Often, and especially during any celebration, he feels safest on the edge or in the next room. This time he was right there, after his birthday meal, in the middle of the sitting room comfortably next to the fireplace, surrounded by friends, newly opened presents and cards and the debris of wrapping paper. A custom such as 'speeches', when we each tell the birthday person how much they have meant to us in the past year, would have been a bit much, so, somewhat riskily, we carried straight on with 'prayers', a time when Patrick often slips off into the kitchen and contemplates a cup of coffee. John, the houseleader, introduced a reading, extracts from a psalm full of the joys and quirkiness of creation, 'the monsters you made to play with', saying how he associated the praise in the psalm with Patrick's sense of wonder and observation. After a brief pause someone thanked God out loud for a funny incident shared with Patrick, then another chipped in with another story, and another with their own thanks and wonder. Patrick sat, smiling broadly, an open can of beer in his hand, surveying all around him. Someone else picked up a guitar and started off 'Do not be afraid, for I have redeemed you; I have called you by your name, you are mine.'

All I give life to
All I give life to, deep in creation
Each word I've spoken, birthing my people
Know that they shall return to me holy
Bearing the life I breathed within, glory.

You who created all of my being
Knit me together, fashioned in secret
Deep in my mother's womb, holy
Sharing the life within, glory.

Rattle the door latch, finding your heart-room
Slumbering heart now filled with elation
Come now lie heartbeat – close to me, holy
Pray in an intimacy free – glory.

l'Arche Edinburgh

In l'Arche communities we often speak of 'welcoming'. We want our homes to be places of welcome, not just to those who have learning disabilities, but also to the assistants who come, often from far away, and to neighbours, friends and visitors. Bit by bit we learn too what it means to let ourselves be welcomed and, hardest of all, to welcome the bits of ourselves we're least proud of. Patrick and I went out to supper one evening to the home of a mutual friend. On the way back we called on some other friends of mine whom Patrick had met before. Patrick mused on each of these friends afterwards: 'They might come, they might come to Liverpool sometime ... we could show them my house ...' In other words he wanted to welcome them, even though in fact he would probably disappear upstairs or to the next room when they came. But he'd be glad and talk about the visit afterwards. So what does it mean for me to be 'welcomed' by Patrick? It doesn't mean that he'd stay and have a conventional conversation over tea and sandwiches. More that he welcomes me into his world. His world of anxieties, fears, hopes, patterns, securities and insecurities. To be welcomed into his world I need to leave a lot of my own agendas behind and just enjoy being there, as on the steps outside the art gallery the other day when we both sat in the sun and Patrick enjoyed his cigarette. Maybe I can only do this if I welcome the weakness within me that my own inner world of anxiety and fear represents.

Relationships can continue and grow, even after we move away from one another in a geographical sense. After spending several years in l'Arche Inverness, Mark Lines became a school teacher and moved to England. But he continued his links with the community through an annual cycling holiday with Syd Fraser, which he describes:

> These trips became voyages of discovery where we grew to know each other better, as well as getting to know Scotland better. We headed north to the coast, taking in Syd's home town of Embo, and west to Ullapool, over to Skye, the Outer Hebrides, and even south to the tip of the Mull of Kintyre. (This was a vain attempt to see Ireland, but due to the cloud we could only just see Scotland!)
>
> One trip was memorable, not only because we discovered a new facet of Scotland, but because of a certain incident. After we'd pushed as far south as we could, we turned round, gratefully receiving help from the wind which made life so hard the day before. It was foggy, and perhaps due too to fatigue, we collided with each other. While we were picking ourselves up we argued. Bizarrely, each of us maintained it was our own fault, and spent a good while apologising.
>
> Our epic voyages are now subjects of endless 'Do you mind the time when . . . ?' conversations. It's an important link between Syd, myself and our common experience.

Holidays nearly always involve journeys, getting to know even the people we live with in new ways, as well as meeting new people. Robert Easton took a break from studies in Oxford to join a group from l'Arche Inverness on holiday in France:

> The fact that we were in a foreign country added a certain 'je ne sais quoi'. Shopping was always interesting; (does 'cheveux' mean hair or horses?) and even a stroll to the post box was far

from dull (is that yellow thing on the wall really a letter box, or perhaps a small French rubbish bin?). Angus became a regular at the village café, while Elaine fell in love with a particularly smelly cheese. Corinne consumed quantities of 'moules frites' and found French TV very educational. Robert enjoyed comparing the nuances of local wines, but it was a local toy museum that brought childhood memories flooding back to James.

Many readers of Chaucer's *Canterbury Tales* today get the impression that his pilgrims were really on what we would call holiday. 'Pilgrimage' can have rather heavy or pious overtones in current language, yet we talk more easily about 'personal journey' or 'journey in life' in a metaphorical sense. Actually pilgrimage is fun as well as challenging – at least as l'Arche communities have discovered it. It's another experience of making real, of acting out, what is happening among us in the daily journey of community life, and of being welcomed and making new friends along the way. Members of l'Arche Lambeth regularly wend their way through the Kent countryside on their way to Canterbury and other communities choose other destinations, finding hospitality in church halls, schools or student chaplaincies on the way.

Pilgrim Song
Called to be one, to share the winding pilgrim road,
Strangers to love, we learn how to forgive;
Welcoming weakness, present in each one of us,
Offered and blessed, now broken to be shared.

l'Arche Edinburgh

Those in l'Arche Liverpool have often chosen Liverpool itself as the 'holy place' for their destination. Beginning far from home in the Lancashire countryside, the community walks by stages, pushing friends in wheelchairs along canal paths and through housing estates to meet with hundreds of members of all the different churches of Merseyside at a joyful ecumenical celebration of Pentecost in Liverpool's two cathedrals. An assistant in the community remarked: 'We needed to go on our pilgrimage; I think we discovered the great gifts we have in the community.' Not everyone can walk the full distance. Needing a lift, or a little help from your friends, is also part of life. Barbara Fraughan can no longer walk as far as she could when she was younger but for her pilgrimage is a joyful and serious business which she gives a glimpse of in her account and drawing. Each of the figures is someone in particular – Barbara is second from the right.

LArche LiveRPooL PiigriMage

We Were Marching in the light of god.
Margaret is carrying the big candle.
There Were treas and grass. They Walked
a long way and the sun Was shining.
The candLle reMindEd me of our Lord Coming
in The clouds.

BarbaraFraughaN

Barbara Fraughan, *l'Arche Liverpool on pilgrimage*

Pilgrimage, journeying together, 'walk on through the wind, walk on through the rain', leaving some of our familiar routines, meeting new people, facing new challenges, needing one another along the way. All of these form a strong image for a way towards unity, reconciliation and the healing of divisions. The very hopeful and historic ecumenical process and commitment initiated by the Churches of Britain and Ireland in Swanwick in 1987 was also called 'No Longer Strangers but Pilgrims Together'. This same theme was taken up in 2002 when the International General Assembly of l'Arche also met at Swanwick and engaged on a three-year process of discernment for the future identity and mission of l'Arche, a process involving all the communities, from different continents, cultures and religious traditions. The song at the end of this chapter was written specially for the Assembly by Australian songwriter John Coleman.[7]

Getting to know one another, building relationships and building places of welcome leads us to ways of healing, to celebrating the uniqueness of each person, to welcoming the presence of Jesus among us in our world. All of these things bring joy and human contact but as the experiences in this chapter have shown, there is a thread of pain as we play and sing 'and take part in the great creative act of life'. This is hardly surprising. Nick Ellerker got it right when he made his drawing of the crucified, reconciling Christ (see chapter 2). We find as we journey that the way to healing and to unity, to fullness of human life, involves loss and letting go. That will be the theme of the next chapter.

No longer strangers but pilgrims together
(Refrain)
No longer strangers but pilgrims together
Called to be woven like threads on the loom

Relate

Drawn by the one God who thirsts for communion
Called by the piper called by the tune.

Though we come from many nations
And our faith has many names
Across oceans over mountains
On these paths of peace we came
To be together in the walking
In the resting in the meal
And when the blessed breath of evening comes
As one the pilgrims kneel.

We know our thirst for God is blessing
We know our hunger's not a curse
We know our emptiness is sacred room
Like a precious spirit purse.
We are lovers of communion
We are building with our clay
A house for God to dwell with us
Let us be the house we pray.

Every thread that's sewn is different
There are no two quite the same
And all the colours make strange rainbows
God's promises made plain.
We submit to the great weaver
Let our pattern be the weaver's refrain
Our God the God of difference
Calls each of us by name.

CHAPTER FOUR
Relinquish

Unless a grain of wheat falls to the ground and dies,
it remains a single grain;
but if it dies it bears much fruit.

John 12:24

WE ALL KNOW THAT LOSS, pain and death are part of life. We witness the suffering of other people every day and sooner or later we each experience loss in our own lives. But how can such pain and letting go possibly bring new life? Many of us invest a lot of energy in defending ourselves, or our self-image, fearfully denying or avoiding our own limitations. Anthony Kramers of l'Arche Edinburgh says:

> The acceptance of weakness is a test of the quality of relationships in community. I fear that a true encounter with the other person will reawaken my own experiences of weakness and loss. And it does. As we walk together on Good Friday, following the way of the cross over the grassy Links in Leith, I find myself remembering recent moments of weakness that people in the community experienced: disappointment over

hoped-for college places, sadness over a parent finding another reason this year not to come to a birthday party, unfulfilled hopes when a friendship broke down in a decision not to marry, the self-questioning of someone else about their sexual identity. And my own painful uncertainty over whether we could as a community renew our commitment to one of the people we had welcomed, who had been going through so many disturbed patches recently. We bring our weaknesses to this way of the cross, moving across the grass and under the trees, as the blossom is tugged by the wind, and children play in the sun.

When the darkness fell on earth
And my people rejected me
I cried 'I thirst': I needed presence and company
When you raised me on the tree
I called each one to stand with me
On holy ground – to touch my body with dignity.

And Jesus said 'I love you',
'Here in my heart take root'
And Jesus said 'I love you: be true.'

Give me water now to drink from the well of your stony heart
And I will strike to free the waters within you
Waters welling up from the body they pierced
Seen mixed with blood, my life is poured out in faithful love.

Song from l'Arche Edinburgh

Learning to love means learning to let go. Loving and letting go are vital ingredients in all relationships and so in community life too, especially in the least glamorous moments. Many of the stories told about life in l'Arche involve relationships with people with disabilities but of course it's among assistants that some of the toughest conflicts arise. Jim Cargin had lived in l'Arche communities for many years and carried a lot of responsibility for l'Arche nationally when he went through the 'important personal experience' that he describes candidly:

> I was supposed to be the more experienced co-ordinator, and John was the 'new kid', so I was keen to show him my skills, whatever that meant to me at the time. I suppose I felt quite threatened and needed to prove myself. Well, by the end of the second day of our first meeting with the others I realised that I was exhausting myself with all this trying to keep up appearances of competence, so I asked John if we could talk. In tears I told him what I had been trying to do . . . then we were able to share very honestly. That graced moment of shared weakness was the basis of much crucial support in the team in the years ahead. Team work based on shared strengths is fine, but we are only in communion with one another when we accept our limitations and let go of our pride.

This sharing of weakness is celebrated in a very tangible way in each l'Arche community during Holy Week, the week before Easter. For Maggie Smith of l'Arche Kent this is a moment of knowing weakness in herself as well as in others:

> I've found that *I* am one of those brothers and sisters that I'm called to live with. I am called to live a covenant with my own weakness and poverty. So much of me seeks to avoid this. It is hard to accept just how needy I am, and to recognise the parts of me that crave affection and affirmation. Those close to me have to bear who I am.

Each year, on the Thursday in Holy Week, the community comes together to enter the mystery of Easter. We recall the year we have just lived together, and then we do as Jesus did. Bending low before each other we wash each other's feet. It's precisely in those parts of me where I least accept myself that Jesus seems to want to meet me. He wants to meet me and he wants me to let myself be met there by my brothers and sisters. 'If I do not wash you, you can have no part in me.' He wants to meet me there so that I can become part of him, of his body. And in the community we seek to meet each other there so that together we can truly become a body that is holy.

In Matthew, Mark and Luke there are definite and very similar accounts of Jesus' meal with his disciples the night before his death. The Last Supper when 'Jesus took a loaf of bread, and after blessing it he broke it, gave it to the disciples and said, "Take, eat, this is my body." Then he took a cup and after giving thanks he gave it to them, saying, "Drink from it all of you; for this is my blood of the covenant, which is poured out for many for the forgiveness of sins"' (Matt. 26). This solemn meal has been passed on and celebrated through two millennia of church history as the sacrament of the Eucharist or holy communion.

However, in the fourth gospel, that of St John, there is no mention of bread and wine at the last meal together but, 'Having loved his own who were in the world, he loved them to the end. During supper Jesus, knowing that the Father had given all things into his hands, and that he had come from God and was going to God, got up from the table, took off his outer robe, and tied a towel around himself. Then he poured water into a basin and began to wash the disciples' feet and to wipe them with the towel that was tied around him. He came to Simon Peter, who said to him "Lord, are you going to wash my feet?" Jesus answered, "You do not know now what I am doing, but later you will understand." Peter said to him, "You will never wash my feet!" Jesus answered, "Unless I wash you, you have no share in me"' (John 13:1b, 3–8).

Many commentaries have explained how it was the duty of a slave to wash the feet of their owners and of guests who arrived, their feet hot and dirty from walking on the dusty roads. Yet Jesus, whom they called 'Lord', stripped and knelt and washed the feet of his unreliable, often squabbling, disciples. In l'Arche communities there is further meaning, since touching and the care of one another's bodies is at the basis of our relationships and our daily life together. Chris Sadler describes her own experience one year in l'Arche Lambeth:

> We began the celebration of Holy Thursday after lunch. We read together the passage in St Mark's gospel when the disciples asked Jesus 'Where do you want us to prepare the Passover?' Then we shared out the tasks of preparing. Philip and I offered to get the sitting room ready for the washing of the feet, finding towels, plastic bowls, soap, jugs of water. Some prepared the festive table, others gathered the 'props' for the story of the Exodus that we would enact during the meal (a crepe paper Red Sea to flounder through, a stick for Moses etc.). Some cooked the meal. There was a sense of quiet purpose and unity as we worked.
>
> The foot washing is always very special. Several people in our house need almost total help in washing and bathing, every day. On this day when roles will be reversed or shared, they seem to sense both the solemnity and the humour of the situation. I love it too, watching Sunta as she pats and laughs over an assistant's foot poised awkwardly on her lap, before she pushes it away as though to say 'Enough, you're done!'

Relinquish

I was asked to begin, washing Philip's feet. As I knelt before him afterwards, he rested his hand on my head. His prayer for me means so much, partly because he is such a faithful man of prayer all the time, all the year, and partly because we have shared so much over the years – little moments which we both found gentle or perhaps amusing; big moments as when his mother died, my friend died or when someone special to us moved from our house. Then I watched him wash Brother Thierry's feet, and was in awe because they have shared an even longer story together. This sense of a thousand, thousand unspoken memories was almost visible in the way they related.

Last in the circle, Terry laboured to the floor to wash my feet. He puffed and groaned but concentrated with a rare intensity. He used soap, rubbing and rubbing, a bit like the way he draws a picture; hand and eye seemingly unconnected, but heart full of feeling. I know how much he suffers from the breakage of routine. I sensed the anxiety which must hang over the next few days for him. Yet he rested quietly as I placed my hands on his head to pray and say 'thank you'.

I feel tears of wonder, which hold the pain and the beauty, the simplicity and the mystery of our lives washed in this love and commandment of Jesus.

Now the shadows grow long, when you rise from the feast
And you strip to the waist, and then fall on your knees
In a loving embrace cradle each person's feet
Water poured on, to heal, to celebrate.

l'Arche Edinburgh

I washed Thierry's feet. When Thierry prayed for me I felt happy. I felt he was praying for me and my family. I know Thierry very well. I used to work in the workshop with him. We've been on pilgrimages together. When I washed his feet I was thinking that I was his friend. It felt nice when Chris washed my feet. Then I prayed for her. I prayed that she was a beautiful, peaceful, faithful person. When my feet are washed it tickles. I like washing the other person's feet most. When I do it for someone else I feel very clean. *I feel happy when we wash each other's feet because we do it to one another, we do it to be friends. It helps us to be together, to live together.*

Philip Yates

As Jesus offered the broken bread to his disciples at the last supper he said 'Do this in remembrance of me' (Luke 22:19.) After he had washed his disciples' feet Jesus said again 'Do this . . . and you will be blessed . . . if I, your Lord and teacher have washed your feet, you also ought to wash one another's feet' (John 13:14). Both actions reveal Jesus' self-giving love and both carry the instruction 'do this'. 'Do this' means our lives, our relationships, those moments Chris recalled as she watched Philip and Brother

Thierry. We may also wash the feet of those we don't get on with ('Oh not her, whom I've been arguing with all week!'). In our churches 'do this' also means meeting Jesus in the sacrament of the bread and wine, bringing our lives and our attempts to love, our needs to forgive and to be forgiven, to the altar.

In l'Arche communities in Britain and elsewhere we are often from different Christian denominations and cannot all receive holy communion from the same table, as the painful experiences of the last chapter told. The sacrament of unity, in which we take part in our parishes and within our communities, is also at times a moment of disunity and contradiction. But we can wash one another's feet together, and we find a strong sacramental aspect in this 'do this'; washing one another's feet is our prayer for unity, our prayer for forgiveness and healing, not just for ourselves and our community, but for the world of which we are part. After he had washed the feet of his friends, Jesus prayed for them and for his future followers 'that they may all be one. As you Father are in me and I am in you, may they also be in us, so that the world may believe that you have sent me.' (John 17)

The Last Supper took place the night before Jesus died. It was his testimony, his way of 'explaining' why he would let himself be taken, tortured and crucified. And so the day after we wash one another's feet, we re-enact Jesus' trial and journey to the cross, culminating in his death on Good Friday. Philip Yates tells of his experience as members of l'Arche Lambeth acted out Jesus' way to the cross, going to each community house in turn:

> We began at the Sycamore. Jesus was condemned to death. Andrew was Jesus. I felt very sad. I felt sorry for Jesus when the soldiers pushed him.
>
> We came back to Gothic Lodge. Simon of Cyrene picked up the cross. James was Simon of Cyrene. He helped Jesus

Philip Yates

carry the cross. Last year I was Simon of Cyrene. I picked the cross up on my shoulder. When Simon walks behind Jesus he thinks about Jesus; he becomes Jesus' friend.

Then we were quiet, and went to the Elmstone. The women wept for him. Jesus went up the steps to the workshop and fell twice. I felt upset. The women wiped his face; they cleaned it. One of the women was Jesus' mother, Mary. She was weeping because Jesus was going to be crucified.

Then we went to the Mustard Seed. They stripped his clothes off. They put a crown of thorns on his head because he was Jesus, the King of the Jews.

We went to the Vine. There they crucified him. They nailed him to the cross. They took him down from the cross and laid him in the shed at the bottom of the garden.

In the evening in the Vine we had the cross on the floor in the living room. The people are on the floor, sitting round the cross. When I was praying near the cross I thought of my mother, and Anne-Marie, and Betty's and Sunta's mother, who have died. I prayed for them – that they would be happy in heaven. I put my head on the cross. I thought Jesus was gone and I felt very sad. I don't know why death is important, but it is.

It was not obvious to Jesus' disciples how his brutal death could bring healing or hope; all they saw and felt was pain and failure. We all live with the same questions. Sometimes it is just that, living with the questions when intellectual processing does not shed much light. A sense of wonder and a capacity to accept mystery, beautiful or painful, can take us deeper. Thérèse Vanier writes of this gift that she has found in the lives of many people with learning disabilities:

The ability to 'accept' mystery is a sure way of finding meaning to life. Only by the acceptance of mystery can one possibly reconcile faith in a loving God with, say, the death of a child or young person. It is a matter of accepting something which is a scandal and needs to be recognised as such, while trusting that somehow, at some time, the meaning of this mystery will be revealed. Those who have been able to integrate experiences of loss into their lives alongside their experience of dependence have acquired a certain wisdom and peace. They have acquired an exceptional ability to trust and to relate to God and to others.[8]

Such acceptance comes at a price. Eva Skeels described her own story in terms of crosses. After more than ten years in l'Arche Lambeth her worsening epilepsy and increasing anguish meant that she had to return to hospital and she now lives in another home where she can receive the nursing and care she needs. The friendship with Marcella Roe that Eva refers to continues. Here is Eva's story:

> I don't always find it easy to talk about when I was a child because of the painful things which have happened in my life. There are many kinds of crosses and sufferings. I shared my story with the community one Good Friday. Marcella helped me to share it because she has known me since I came to l'Arche and has lived with me longer than any other assistant in my house. It is not easy to share, but it is not good to keep the painful things bottled up inside, because that way it feels hard like a stone inside your heart.
>
> When I was four and a half years old I was knocked down by a car and taken to hospital. The doctors and nurses were very kind to me. They didn't think I would live. I love doctors and nurses and hospitals ever since. This was the beginning of my disability, because I was left with a learning disability and epileptic fits. Sometimes this makes me very angry when I think about the accident, because I can't do all the things other people can do; it makes me feel I am different. I couldn't do the things my brothers and sisters could do when I was a child, or understand things in the same way. When this happened everyone got annoyed and impatient with me. I was a big problem to my mother who didn't always know how to manage me and my fits. I hated school because the teachers weren't understanding. The other children teased me and laughed at me and I preferred to be on my own and not talk to anyone.

My Dad left and went to New Zealand and I never saw him again. Then I had to leave home and come to l'Arche and live away from my Mum. Leavings are hard for me. I have had a lot of leavings. I was very jealous when the assistants I lived with left at different times to get married and to have children. This made me angry, because I wanted to get married and to have a child, but that didn't happen for me, and still hasn't happened for me. My boyfriend left me and walked out on me. This felt like a tree branch being broken, snapped, so that you can't put it back together again like it was before. Something is broken inside you; your heart is broken.

Some good things have happened for me in l'Arche. I have work I like doing and am good at in the stone work and making candles and I have friends. I don't go to church but friends in l'Arche help me. I always pray for poor children who have no food. I am telling you about my crosses and crosses are different for different people.

Crosses are different for different people. Frances Young is a Methodist minister, a university professor of theology and the mother of Arthur, a man with severe learning disabilities. She was invited to join a Faith and Light pilgrimage to Lourdes during Holy Week. Faith and Light is a sister organisation to l'Arche, bringing together people with learning disabilities, their families and friends, in non-residential communities that share and celebrate and pray together. Faith and Light, like l'Arche, is ecumenical but it is a brave Methodist who joins a pilgrimage to Lourdes! For Frances there were many new experiences, outward, 'cultural' differences like the stations of the cross, the processions and of course the statues of Mary, the mother of Jesus. But there was also something more important, as she struggled at many levels.

On Good Friday morning, Mervyn's mum was going to bathe in the spring water. I decided to go with her. The rapid dip in the ice-cold water was exhilarating. No towels were provided, since the lime-saturated water rapidly dries. I emerged disappointed that my hands and my face had not entered the water as the attendants lowered and raised me. I knew that I should have to go to the taps and wash my face. But there was no time. We had to meet our group to follow the stations of the cross. I was to read the scriptures for the crucifixion scene. We all mimed the hammering of the nails, and we all cried out with Jesus, 'My God, my God, why hast thou forsaken me?'

Later that day, after the massive crowds of the Good Friday services, I escaped on my own, and took the steep path up the hill. There the most amazing series of sculptures, bronze and more than life-size, depict the stations of the cross in full. It was a tough climb, not recommended for the disabled or for wheelchairs. As I mounted I surprised myself as I began to be deeply moved and to weep at visual art in a way that only music, like Bach's *St Matthew Passion*, has previously aroused in me. With the women of Jerusalem I brought my child to the suffering, struggling Christ as he stumbled carrying the cross, and I begged a blessing. In identity with Mary I met my innocent, suffering son and felt the pain of the sword piercing the mother's heart. The tears streamed, and when I reached the top of the hill, I couldn't gaze at the Calvary. The afternoon sun was in my eyes, dazzling and blinding. Lining up the cross to cut the glare, all I could see were dark silhouettes. It was as though I were literally experiencing the paradox of Christ's exposure to the darkness of the world's sin and suffering which St John's gospel calls the hour of glory.

But then I followed the path around behind, and was amazed how, looking the other way, having passed behind the cross, Calvary became illuminated, bright and clear – and the tears were dried and the sound of cow-bells floated up from the meadow below. My eyes were opened to the grace which takes away our darkness, and peace began to dawn. Over the hill, cleverly placed before a natural fissure in the rock was the final scene, a group bringing the body to lay it in the tomb.

I returned from my lonely struggle to community. But the end was not yet. Good Friday evening, meeting with the group of English speakers to meditate on suffering and to pray, to listen to testimonies, to sing the Taizé chant, 'Stay here, remain here with me, watch and pray', like all the other mums in the place, I guess, not to mention some dads, I was again reduced to tears. It was that tough place where I know that, with the best intentions in the world, I have let Arthur down. It was Francis, one of the disabled men in our group, who held my hand, and afterwards we went, just the two of us, to the Grotto. Francis is an old hand – he's been to Lourdes eight times. Together we touched and kissed the wet rock, and I perceived something of the importance of that elemental touching – especially for people who find mental conception difficult. Together we wondered in silence at the spring of pure water, and I acknowledged its beauty and mystery. Then we went to the taps, and Francis washed my face. My tears were purified. I washed his face and together we cupped our hands and drank.

That night in my weakness I was convinced that I should be with my new friends in community for the Easter Vigil – I hadn't the strength for ministry. But in the event circumstances demanded obedience, and on Holy Saturday ministry was required of me. So I found yet again that my healing comes from obedience to that call. I could speak from a place of deep truth about transformation, and then on Easter Sunday proclaim a resurrection that makes a real difference to our lives.

We cannot come to unity without healing and forgiveness, and we cannot receive healing and forgiveness without being present in some way to what the cross of Jesus represents – touching pain, letting go of pride or power or whatever separates us from one another, from God, from our deepest selves.

Frances Young's experience illustrates the way of the cross and healing and her poem ends this chapter.

Mary, my child's lovely.
Is yours lovely too?
Little hands, little feet.
Curly hair, smiles sweet.

Mary, my child's broken.
Is yours broken too?
Crushed by affliction,
Hurt by rejection,
Disfigured, stricken,
Silent submission.

Mary, my heart's bursting.
Is yours bursting too?
Bursting with labour, travail and pain.
Bursting with agony, ecstasy, gain.
Bursting with sympathy, anger, compassion.

Mary, my heart's joyful.
Is yours joyful too?

CHAPTER FIVE
Receive

I could speak from a place of deep truth
about transformation, and then on Easter
Sunday proclaim a resurrection that makes a real
difference to our lives.

Frances Young

WE LET GO, OUR HANDS are empty, so how and what do we receive, in our lives and in our relationships? What does this have to do with Easter, the resurrection and our longing for unity?

Like Frances Young, Karen Cowburn is the mother of a learning-disabled child. Her daughter, Emma, is a founding member of l'Arche in Preston. When a woman is pregnant she is said to be 'expecting'. Expecting a baby, yes. But expecting much more, all the hope and promise of the child's future. Karen Cowburn describes how she's learned to let go of expectations and much more and instead receive.

I well remember seeing our second child for the very first time; her hands were so tiny, and yet even then her fingers were long and slender. 'Could she be our concert pianist?' we wondered. High hopes and dreams for the future years, but

other expectations seemed almost to be taken for granted –
our right even. That she would learn to crawl, walk, talk, like her
brother, then two years old and talkative. That she would grow
from totally dependent babyhood through the stages of
toddler, child, adolescent, following our chosen path of
education to become – who knows? And that my role as her
mother would pass through phases too, from carer in the early
years to, I hoped, confidante and friend, as she became a
woman in her own right.

When shortly after her birth we learned that Emma's
brain had been damaged we were shattered. We no longer
dared to look into the future, there were no certainties any
more. We learned to live day by day, week by week. We
belonged to a whole new world now, one that included many
doctors, psychologists, specialist teachers, and also other
parents and families with a disabled child. One of the many
gifts Emma has brought to our lives is the people we have
met because of her.

However, parents of disabled children also share a fear,
often unspoken, but almost always there: 'who will care for our
daughter or son when we're no longer here, or no longer able
to?' As Emma reached the end of her school years, when she
had blossomed and developed her own confident and
infectious personality, we felt we needed to face this fear. As
we thought and searched we realised that it wasn't about
'how?' or 'where?' but 'with whom?'. Not facilities and
programmes but people and relationships. We were looking for
our and, more importantly, Emma's way forward.

Letting go is probably the hardest and ultimately the most
unselfish thing that we as parents can do for our children. Emma's
move to l'Arche was made bearable only by our conviction
that life within l'Arche offered opportunities that we could not

provide, and that we would still be able to share in those experiences.

Emma has a life of her own now and is most definitely a young woman in her own right. With love and support she is enabled to live as independently as she can. As I am freed of my role of personal carer, begun almost 20 years ago, I am able to enjoy a mother-daughter relationship that I never dreamed would be possible; to call in and share a meal, or just a cup of tea and a chat, is extraordinary in its ordinariness – normal even.

Karen and Emma Cowburn

Risen Lord
Give us a heart for the simple things,
Love, laughter, bread and wine and dreams,
Give us a green, growing hope
And make of us a people whose song is 'alleluia',
Whose name is love, whose sign is peace,
Whose name is love, whose sign is peace.

Song from l'Arche Edinburgh

It may seem strange to describe the deaths of community members in a chapter about receiving new life. Yet amid the loss and grieving and mutual letting go, those are the moments where we have truly experienced Easter. In the second chapter Sue Jones described George Munnerley's journey in l'Arche Liverpool. It was a journey, often painful, into life and also into letting go of this life.

> During his difficult years George would often talk about his fear of illness and death, of 'going down the hole in a box', and was bitterly afraid of the local undertakers getting hold of his money. But during his last years George had learned to live again; he had learned to receive and give love, he had learned to laugh and he had discovered a home, friends and a family. So great was his transformation in his last three or four years that he was able to live his final illness with us peacefully and well.
>
> When George did become ill with cancer the most difficult time was his operation and the week he spent in hospital. He was very afraid of being left there, of not coming home. Right from the start the community had decided that George should know the truth of his illness, so he was never told that he would get better, only that he would certainly be coming

home. When he came home from hospital his downstairs room wasn't ready, so he had a bed in the living room, as a temporary measure. But once established at the centre of the house with life going on around him, he didn't want to move, so he stayed there for the next two months. During that time he became gradually weaker but he decided his own rhythm of life. He got up when he wanted, if he felt like a walk to the workshop or the shops then he would go. He got into bed after supper and rested while everyone else in the house talked, sang and said prayers around his bed in the evening. George enjoyed his visitors who streamed in, surrounding him with love and tenderness. He knew he was getting weaker and gradually he said goodbye to all his functions and jobs. One day he said 'I won't be going to the workshop any more' and another day 'someone else will put the milk bottles out'.

After those two peaceful months it was clear that the noise and the activity in the living room were becoming too tiring for George and he asked to move into the bedroom downstairs. Friends, family and the community made a rota of people to sit with George and he was never alone. For those who sat with him and cared for him this was a time of great grace. A candle burned at the bedside. George was struggling to come to terms with his impending death. He began talking about not wanting to go down the hole in a box, and he was assured that although his body would be buried he would not be there. The next time he was washed George looked down at himself and said 'this is my body'. He asked for a mirror and looked long and hard at his face, and then put the mirror away.

His dignity and determination taught us all and we found our faith challenged and purified by the experience of being with George. We couldn't tell George that he was on his way to eternal life without believing this ourselves. In the presence of his gentleness and weakness many of us found ourselves powerfully in the presence of God and participating in a great mystery.

George died early one morning. The others in the community were told as they got up and everyone came, gathering around his body for prayer. It was a moment of great unity. The funeral was a wonderful rousing celebration of joy and sadness. George's Baptist Pastor told us that 'George has not got into heaven by his coat tails, but he has conquered and is now living in glory!'

Later Susan was able to reflect on the experience:

George gave us incredible gifts in the way he died. He enabled all of us to face our own fears about death and showed us how to die well. Those who lived the experience with him became wonderfully bonded together as a new and stronger community. I am so grateful that George had made a passage from death to life in his early years in the community, a passage that enabled him to let go and make another passage to true fullness of life.

The year George died was my first year of l'Arche life, though I'd already known George and the community for some time. I was so struck by the love everyone felt for George. At his funeral I was struck by the packed church and the resurrection hope expressed as we celebrated the life and death of this anything but pious man who, had I met him ten years earlier, I'd have described as 'down and out'. George had received life and had drawn others around him into life.

I met Keith Lindsay at his home, the 'Sycamore' in l'Arche

Lambeth. Keith had no speech but could certainly communicate. Over the dining room in the Sycamore there is a sky light. The flight path from Heathrow often crosses this part of South East London and as we sat at table for the evening meal in winter Keith enjoyed spotting the lights as planes flew over. He was a wonderfully creative person and his paintings were shown in a London gallery and turned into greeting cards. Keith was also an enthusiastic photographer. Keith died very suddenly one night just before Christmas. The community was stunned. Friends who were contacted included Andrew Laing, who spoke about his friendship with Keith at Keith's funeral:

> The news that Keith had died was shocking. Totally unexpected. Keith was a one-off in every way. My first encounter with him was the day I came to visit l'Arche as a prospective assistant nearly five years ago. There was I, the new assistant, eager to please. There was Keith, the wise old community member who wasn't embarrassed to have me spending two hours unravelling his knitting.
>
> Over the next few years we did a lot of things together. We visited the Alps and sailed on Lake Constance, we took part in pilgrimages, drama workshops and faith sharing groups, and we cooked and drank and laughed together. Keith even had a flying lesson during a visit to my home town in Scotland. Take it from me – when you're in a small plane that's circling a mile up in the air and it's being controlled by Keith Lindsay ... let's just say I knew what it was to feel intensely alive!
>
> We visited Rome together and even met the Pope, though the highlight for Keith was the pasta at lunchtime – Keith always liked his food! Keith loved life even though it had not always been kind to him. He could enjoy more happiness from one little thing that interested him than anyone else I've met.

Keith Lindsay, *London Bus*

Keith was faithful too. Every day he came downstairs to the kitchen and crossed the day off on the calendar. And if it was your birthday he'd head back upstairs and the next thing you'd hear would be his keyboard clattering off the walls as he carried it downstairs. He would rig it all up in the kitchen and play 'Happy Birthday'.Then he would cheer and tidy it all away again. He was faithful to his work in the workshop, he worked hard. He was faithful too to his printing class. He was faithful to worshipping in this beautiful church. And he was faithful to his friends.

He was so faithful that I received a hand made Christmas card from him four days after he died! It set me thinking though – if Keith could send us a card today, what would it be like? On the front there would probably be a photograph of

Jesus, whether Jesus had wanted his picture taken or not! And inside Keith would want to say 'Don't worry. I'm more myself now than I've ever been.'

When he was alive Keith would sit in the Sycamore looking up at the roof and laughing away to himself – you might think he was seeing angels that no one else could. Well if he wasn't then he certainly is now, because I think we may be confident that Keith is rejoicing in the embrace of unbelievable love that we call heaven.

Easter blessing
Taken down from the tree, you are laid on her breast,
And the body they pierced christens now her distress.
On the day of the dead you descend to the gloom
Softly greeting – by name – with tenderness.

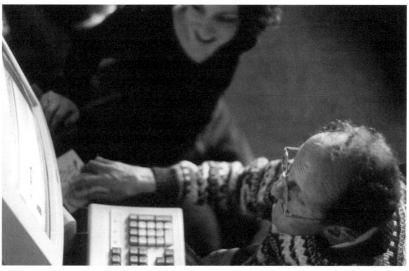

Keith Lindsay

Mary runs to the tomb, her eyes blinded with grief,
Tears are full in her face, as the dawn lights the gloom.
Meeting him whom she knows, in a loving embrace,
'Do not cling to me now but celebrate'.

l'Arche Edinburgh

L'Arche communities celebrate Easter, the resurrection of Jesus, with mimes, symbols and festivities, as well as taking part in local church liturgies. How to express this gift of new life? Can any of us understand or absorb the wonder of Easter? We can understand death and pain but what does it mean to come back from the dead? That Jesus did not just turn the clock back, to make it all better after all, but that he conquered death by death? So many of us are like the two travellers to Emmaus at the end of Luke's gospel, exhausted by the events and grief of Holy Week and touched by scepticism and disillusion. We too have another journey to make before our eyes are opened and our 'hearts burn within us'. Sometimes it's just that – a journey from head understanding to heart understanding. People who live less in their heads than their hearts can give us pointers. How do children receive the life-changing news of Easter? L'Arche communities include families, often with young children. Marguerite Kramers describes Easter with her family and in the Edinburgh community when her daughter Kirsten wasn't yet five years old.

What to say of
'Holy Saturday'

This day of emptiness
The day in the tomb
The day of
No liturgy.

Our domestic liturgy includes noticing that the crocuses have
died as we cross the Links with Kirsten. 'Why did they die?' she
asks, and is eager to point out those which are still alive. We
burn the soup at lunchtime.

In the afternoon Kirsten is very out of sorts and, unusually,
sleeps a long heavy sleep. 'Is Kirsten ill?' we wonder. 'When
will she rise again?'

> Late in the evening
> We are bathed
> In the first light
> Fire
> Easter vigil.

Easter Sunday

> Our table bears three gifts of new life –
> a candle
> bread
> a vase of daffodils.

Kirsten's face absorbs each of these in turn as she faces
them in at her eye level. She has recovered, and asks for a
piece of the Easter bread that we had made together earlier in
the week. Happy Easter!

After church we go to one of the community houses for
lunch. Kirsten and Bertie are laughing. 'Boing!' she shrieks. It's
good to be together again!

The whole community gathers with some friends. After
hearing the gospel story of the empty tomb, Valerie tells us
why eggs are used at Easter, reminding us of new life and of
the stone which had been rolled away. 'Claire and Kirsten' she

says 'would you like to give everyone an egg to decorate?'
Together and very slowly they take the basket of eggs round
the whole room. In fact they remind me now of 'the two men
in brilliant clothes (who) suddenly appeared' (Luke 24:4). In
their action they are saying to us all 'Take an egg, touch it, the
stone has been rolled away', like those other two said 'Why
look among the dead for someone who is alive?' (Luke 24:5).

Life goes on but is new, different. In the previous chapter we
processed with members of l'Arche Lambeth as they followed the
cross from house to house. The whole world was present as they
shared stories of suffering. Hope spread to the whole world too
through more images and story telling on Easter day, a day that
ended on a domestic note, as Louise Heatley recalls:

In the evening of Easter Sunday we celebrated our final paschal
liturgy – the blessing of light. We lit our Easter candle and took
it from room to room, welcoming the light of the risen Christ
into our home as well as into our hearts. I love this liturgy. It is
the moment in the year when I am most aware of that which
is sacred touching the ordinariness of our lives. As our straggly
little procession of a dozen people moves through the house
singing 'the light of Christ has come into the world', so we
give thanks for our surroundings, and all that makes up our
daily life. We pray for the meals we eat, the meetings we have,
our rest, our play, our prayer. We give thanks for our home – as
Sylvia says, 'My room. Amen. Nice curtains. Amen. New carpet.
Amen . . .' – and for the life we share. The days of Easter invite
me to know that Christ is risen, and so my life has meaning. As
I recall that life, with its struggles, joys and sorrow, I give great
thanks for what I'm called to live and the sisters and brothers
I've been given.

Perhaps many of us have celebrated Easter too many times to experience the terror and confusion, and the joy, that the women at the tomb must have gone through. We've read the story too often to understand. Theologian James Alison offers help when he draws attention to the parallel with the story of the angels coming to announce good news to Sarah and Abraham, a couple who each thought they were much too old for the news to be credible. Sarah's reaction to the promise that she would have a child was first laughter (don't be stupid!) and then fear, fear of the unforeseen, a promise for the future that would change everything. So too, the reaction of the women at Jesus' tomb was confusion and fear before joy. As with Sarah, nothing in their existing understanding could interpret what was beginning to dawn, that God had opened up a future beyond any expectation, transcending death, and from which there was no escape route back into security. Terrifying.

Terrifying and joyful. Through her painful but hopeful journey of letting go and of being ministered to, Frances Young was able to proclaim the Easter message with conviction to the thousands of people gathered at Lourdes. She goes on to describe the end of that Faith and Life pilgrimage, when Jesus with Down's Syndrome simply and powerfully challenged the Church leaders to pray and work for unity:

> Easter Monday. Sun streaming out of a blue sky on a vast crowd with colourful banners, 20,000 odd, half of them mentally disabled. Over the microphone sounds a voice, in English, then French, then Spanish.
>
> 'On the first day of the week Mary Magdalene came to the tomb.'
>
> Dressed in blue, a woman with learning disabilities, and a friend, appear on the stage and mime the actions.

'It was very early in the morning, still dark. The stone had been rolled away from the tomb. The tomb was empty. Mary was very sad. She stood outside the tomb crying, "They have taken away my Lord and I do not know where they have laid him."'

A chap with Down's Syndrome appears wrapped in a cloak.

'She turned round and saw Jesus standing there. She didn't know it was Jesus. She thought it was the gardener. Jesus asked, "Woman, why are you weeping? Whom do you seek?"'

The woman playing Mary falls to her knees.

'Mary said to him, "Sir, if you have carried him away, tell me where you have laid him and I will take him away." And Jesus said, "Maria".'

Jesus raises his arms. The cloak falls from his shoulders to reveal his white robe. He takes Mary's hands and lifts her.

'And Mary said, "Rabuni!" Jesus said, "Go and tell my brothers."'

He points out a group in the corner of the stage. Mary goes and fetches them.

'I have seen the Lord. Come and see!'

They kneel before Jesus. Then Jesus lifts each up and embraces them in turn, first a woman Methodist minister, then a Cardinal, then a Catholic Bishop, then an Anglican Bishop.

'He says to them, "Love one another as I have loved you."'

They embrace each other, and then in Italian, French, English and Spanish the church representatives say, 'Let us pray that we may be one in the love of Jesus.' And 20,000 people shared the peace.

In the last three chapters we have followed a search for unity and for community from the stages of relating and journeying together, through letting go and bearing pain, and then to receiving hope and renewed relationships through resurrection. It's all been very ordinary and at times messy, as all our lives are. In l'Arche communities we describe the new deeper relationships that are given to us through this journey as 'covenant relationships'. Covenant is an old biblical word that has come to mean various things today, even agreements with the Inland Revenue! In the next and final chapter we'll explore a little what God-given covenant means in the light of the death and resurrection of Jesus, in the experience of l'Arche and in a wider context, a context of reconciliation and hope among our churches and beyond.

Meanwhile this resurrection chapter ends with a song of hope from l'Arche Edinburgh, based on one of George Mackay Brown's last poems 'Good Friday to Easter'.

Drifts of Apple Blossom

Down and round he went, his lantern a star
Clothed in his five wounds, to meet in the gloom,
Daffodil-coated, greeting him with a kiss
Solomon the wise, the Son of Man in tryst.

Down and down he went, to songs of the harp
There upon the step the shepherd-king cries,
Down at the root, the Tree of Man disguised
Dust of apple blossom fills the urn of life.

Digger of life in the garden
Yearning for hallelujah,
Day of the dead now yields to hope of spring
Apple blossom drifting o'er the servant-king.

Deeper down lay Joseph, counsellor of kings
Blessing o'er the Son, who Bread of life now brings
Turning he comes, now hailed upon the step
Angel-wrestler meets, whose stone with oil had wept.

Flute and fleeces Abel foregathering
He who bore the wound, the first entombed by lust
Seventh step down, the tall and primal dust
Turned with a cry, from digging, delving.

Fisher of life in the garden
Yearning for hallelujah,
Day of the dead now yields to hope of spring
Apple blossom drifting o'er the servant-king.

CHAPTER SIX
Covenant, in Christ

'What life have you if you have not life together?'

T. S. Eliot

THIS QUESTION FROM T. S. Eliot in 'Choruses from "The Rock"' would certainly not have been in Ian Watkinson's mind when he repeatedly talked about 'my life together ... together' when we were on pilgrimage to Iona (described in the Introduction). For Ian it wasn't a question, but more an affirmation of what he was experiencing about himself and being together in community. T. S. Eliot wrote 'Choruses from "The Rock"' during the Depression of the 1930s, scathingly questioning the effects of competition, materialism, exclusion, and especially in this poem, unemployment. The poem is a call to build, to build church, not just a church building, but community. It continues:

> There is no life that is not in community,
> And no community not lived in praise of God

These lines sound like a big claim, more like Ian's affirmation on Iona. In another sense they express an ideal, an ideal that those of us who try to live in community might say 'yes … but' to. An ideal only believable if we know life to be a gift from God in whom community, communion, is a reality.

Gather in the Gift of our Lives (part 2)
Jesus, we trust you.
Gathered in your name,
you are here among us,
a stranger, Lord and friend.

Washing our feet,
you love through to the end
to transfigure your friends,
to embrace a covenant people.

O Spirit we love you;
Renew our pilgrim hope.
And may we, though many,
become one,
deep in the heart of God.

l'Arche Edinburgh

When I began thinking about this book I was warned to avoid jargon, l'Arche jargon, churchy jargon, the short-hand expressions we fall into when we talk about something a lot … and which then lose their currency. I apologise for those places where I have not succeeded. This book is about unity and 'unity' risks being a jargon word too. A friend challenged me to list all the other words and expressions I might use in its place. St Paul's words on 'unity', writing to the Philippians, are variously translated as 'be united in your convictions, united in your love, with a common purpose' or 'be of the same mind, having the same love, being in full accord and of one mind'. But it is his opening phrase that inspires and names the source of such unity which otherwise would depend on our efforts: 'If our life in Christ means anything to you, if love can persuade at all, or the Spirit that we have in common . . .' (Phil. 2:1, Jerusalem Bible)

'*In* Christ' is a curious expression, without many parallels, although Paul uses it more than thirty times in his letters: 'If anyone is in Christ, there is a new creation: everything old has passed away; see, everything has become new! All this is from God, who reconciled us to himself through Christ, and has given us the ministry of reconciliation' (2 Cor. 5:17–18). St John also speaks of 'dwelling in Christ'. Maybe we are in danger of more jargon. Is '*in* Christ' like being 'in a football team' or '*in* England'? It sounds more like a whole new state of being, the medium in which we live, like living, breathing, moving in water, or being in community, or in love.

Being 'in Christ' affects all our relationships, not because we are setting up something new, but rather realising, making real, what now exists because of Christ; dis-covering, or revealing, our common humanity, and receiving a gift. So there is no need to fall into 'oughts' as we read the next lines in Paul's letter to the Philippians, which can sound unattractive: 'no competition, no conceit, everyone self-effacing, humble'. (Phil. 2:3) This is very worthy and we know it makes sense and strengthens community, but can feel 'not me, not yet . . .' We often fear that unless we are competitive, self-confident and assertive we will lose our self-worth. Paul (who of all people had a very strong ego) is talking about the individualism claimed by the false ego which needs to hand over to our true self in real relationships. We are who we are *in* relationships and belonging, not threatened by them.

This problem of 'oughts' is clearer when Paul is chiding the Christians in Corinth for their disunity. Paul is not saying 'Jesus told us to love each other and to be united; why aren't you doing that?' but rather 'Do you not know that you *are* one in Christ – you are members depending on each other; how can you behave as if you were not?' Then, with the Philippians (2:5), Paul is persuasive again: 'Let the same mind be in you that was in Christ Jesus.' The hymn that follows is that great pattern of relinquishing and receiving that sums up the whole mystery of the incarnation and opens up the possibility of discipleship, of transformation.

> Though he was in the form of God,
> Jesus did not regard equality with God as something to be
>   exploited,
> but emptied himself, taking the form of a slave,
> being born in human likeness.
> And being found in human form, he humbled himself
> and became obedient to the point of death – even death on a
>   cross.
>
> Therefore God also highly exalted him,
> and gave him the name that is above every name,
> so that at the name of Jesus every knee should bend,
> in heaven and on earth and under the earth,
> and every tongue should confess that Jesus Christ is Lord,
> to the glory of God the Father.
>
> *Phil. 2:5–11*

Archbishop Rowan Williams spells out the way that being 'in Christ' changes our relationships, and he links this to changes in power and authority, bringing us back to relinquishing, letting go, to washing one another's feet:

It is not simply that relations of 'love' are established; that would tell us very little. Far more important is Paul's conviction ... that the relation of Christians to each other is one of building up: we are engaged, in Christ, in *constructing* each other's humanity, bringing one another into the inheritance of power and liberty whose form is defined by Jesus. And that form ... is precisely the power that gives authority and assurance to others and the freedom that sets others free ... I am called to use the authority given me by Christ (by Christ's *giving away* of power conceived as control and security) so as to nurture that authority in others, so that they may give it away in turn – to me and to others. So in John 13 what Jesus gives (service) is to be the currency of exchange between believers: to grow into Jesus' 'Lordship' (his freedom from all other powers) is to become able to wash one another's feet, that is, to welcome them as a guest at the same table.[9]

Relations of love in Christ, constructing each other's humanity, washing one another's feet, are expressed here so concisely in theological terms, but for most of us, including surely Rowan Williams, they are only perceived through years of struggling to live together. Some time ago some people for whom l'Arche had become a way of life needed a way to express how relationships with people who may be very different, very dependent or vulnerable, touch us, change us, are of God, *in* God. We began to use the word 'covenant'. 'Covenant relationships' are not one way but mutual; we find that we grow as we journey together through many years or through intense, transforming moments. The hymn from the letter to the Philippians, quoted above, is often read when we celebrate 'covenant' together, with the washing of feet, at the end of particular l'Arche retreats. For Paul, to be 'in Christ' is to be in the risen victim, the killed-but-living one, in whom God has brought about and continues to bring about a new creation, offering forgiveness. This is the experience that this book has tried to trace through the daily stories of relate–relinquish–receive, and is the source of what in l'Arche we call 'covenant'. What does 'covenant' mean in this context? God gave a 'covenant' to his people in the Hebrew testament, through Noah, Abraham and Moses, and symbolised in the account with Noah by a rainbow. Christians understand Jesus as the 'new covenant', as the letter to the Hebrews wonderfully represents. God promises and we receive and respond.

I am the deepest yearning of your heart
I am the deepest yearning of your heart;
I am the covenant of love you will live;
I am the breath of God within your heart;
O listen to my call,
Listen to my call.

l'Arche Edinburgh

John and Louise Redwood met when they were both assistants in l'Arche Inverness. When their first child, Thomas, was baptised, he and his godfather, Derek Thain, a learning-disabled member of the Inverness community, embarked on a sort of covenant journey together, a journey that grows out of the covenant relationship already shared between John, Louise and Derek:

We had our son, Thomas, baptised in January in our parish church in Edinburgh. Derek was an obvious choice for god-father for a number of reasons. He was interested that we were having a baby, and thrilled for us when Thomas was born. Both of us have lived with Derek so we know he prays every day and would pray for Tom. We also know Derek to be a warm, kind and fun person who would enjoy watching his godson grow up.

The day of the baptism did not work out as planned. The minibus could only manage 30 mph on the A9 from Inverness to Edinburgh, so Derek was too late for the service, but he arrived in time to make a speech and thoroughly enjoyed his new status as a godfather.

Derek now visits us, and despite our best efforts to elicit the first laugh from Tom, it was not until he saw Derek take his flat cap off and throw it across the room that Tom laughed properly for the first time!

Baptism is setting out on a journey in Christ, with others. Lizzie Nelson has never been an assistant in a l'Arche community but she has become a member of l'Arche Lambeth, where her husband, Hugh, who she met at university, has lived and worked since they were both students. Lizzie's journey into belonging in the community was a slow one, sometimes difficult in the early days: '. . . An experience of division, the sense that I was always on the outside looking in, and not seen as a person in my own right, but as the partner of someone more real, more present, and me as the threat, the stranger drawing him away . . .' But she persevered, getting to know assistants who were glad of friendship beyond the community houses, and Lizzie enjoyed meal times and prayer times in a l'Arche house: 'The relationship in the Vine, expressed through banana-telephone games at the meal table, and quiet sharing at prayer times, helped me to see a real presence of God in a way I haven't seen or experienced in church.'

Eventually Lizzie was baptised, which she described as 'the fruit of a long journey in which l'Arche Lambeth played an important part'. Primrose Pollock, a learning-disabled member of the Vine, is her godmother.

At my baptism Primrose signed me with the sign of the cross, in oil on my forehead. Primrose never forgets that she's my godmother, and reminds me of my baptism and her gift to me every Sunday in church. So many people from l'Arche Lambeth came to my baptism; I felt held and surrounded, lifted up by this loving community to God. As the service finished Brian stepped forward and gave me an immense Brian hug; again I knew that this was God, through Brian's strong and unwieldy arms, receiving me and welcoming me with joy.

In covenant God gives, gives relationship, with God and so too with one another, but a relationship that waits to be real-ised, to be made real. The relationships between Lizzie and Primrose, and Lizzie and Brian are in God and reveal God, even though Lizzie would not have looked at them in that way as she began to find her place in community. Many couples would describe their marriage as a covenant, their primary place of community. We journey together in many different 'combinations' in families, churches and communities, and covenant relationships are not only one-to-one friendships. Covenant describes something about the source of our knowing, our discovering, and especially our faithfulness, in very diverse relationships. Baska Pestka knew this through her friendship with James Fraser in l'Arche Inverness. James expressed part of what St Paul meant in his letter to the Philippians, quoted above, in one of his short poems:

God's poverty
If you don't have a good feeling in your heart,
You will never know
The poverty of God.

James was a giver and he has given a great deal to the reflection in this book through his poems, his 'warmness' (a word often used in his poems), and his friendship with angels. James died in July 2002, while this book was still in the making, just before he was to go to Poland on holiday to visit his friend Baska.

Baska lived for many years in Inverness where she got to know James. She now leads one of the communities of l'Arche in her native Poland. Baska writes:

> To have known James was a great privilege. The gift of friendship we received in each other and nourished and cherished for 13 years, was one of the most precious in my life. We sparked each other off. We've given life to one another, carried one another through weakness, and shared laughter and joy.

James Fraser

He was a man of great joy, saying, 'There is no point in being sad, because you've got to face the fact of warmness, which is good.' James loved life and has lived his life to its fullness, even till the last day: 'I always pray for another day.' His life, however fragile at times, was a continuing journey of discovering the gifts God had placed in him, which he so generously shared with us. One day when I was going away from Inverness for a few months, James stopped me at the door of Braerannoch, our home, and said, 'I will miss you because you know me and I know you.'

James Fraser, *Angels*

The Moon and the Stars – again
Do you ever watch God?
He's a great guy.

How do I watch him?
I have an angel.

When I look at the moon and the stars
In my bed – when I take my glasses off –
Then it is heaven;
I am in a glorious place.
God is good!

James Fraser

James and Baska, different as they were, built their friendship over many years. If we move on frequently there are many things we will never discover in relationships, many things we will never know about ourselves, especially in areas of forgiveness and reconciliation. Anthony Kramers reflects on this:

Discerned choices to stay or leave, made by each member in freedom, and confirmed by others who know them and love them, both as they are and as the person they could become – these are the mark of community. I have been blessed with many glimpses of this over the years, in my own choices to stay as a single person, and later as a couple and family, and through changes of community and role. I've seen it in the influence of community on the development of children. I've seen it in accompanying others as a witness to their journey, and in leadership.

Most of all I've seen it in the beauty of the wisdom of some of those who have made their home in l'Arche, like

James Fraser, learning-disabled member of l'Arche Inverness with twenty-two years of community experience. A new assistant burst in on him in the kitchen, struggling to contain his fury about a conflict elsewhere, and the impossibility of community. 'Have some tea', said James, a gentle man of art and poetry. 'You know, God has a special love for those who lose their self control . . .'.

We find this sense of 'covenant' in relationships in which we receive and grow, relationships that we can recognise as being 'in God'. Friendships, yes, but friendships in difference, taking us out of ourselves and into our divided, fearful world, as Jim Cargin writes:

L'Arche is one sign, among many thank goodness, that this astonishing covenant is not just wishful thinking, but a visible reality. Perhaps the greatest witness to it is not so much the ordinary friendships that would exist anyway, but those extraordinary friendships that strike up against the norms of society, between people who are on the face of it very different. Something different is happening, scandalous even, and it's a good thing to sit down and think about it, and to realise that friendship across differences, going beyond the expected and the known, is a source of hope. The world desperately needs to come to terms with its diversity, and this won't happen by people just making friends with others who are like themselves; that is too limiting, and now also, far too dangerous. If ever we could afford this luxury we can no longer. Of course we need friends who are like ourselves, but now as never before, we need to venture further, for what the world needs is faith in the possibility that we, in all our rich and threatening diversity, can live together, in peace.'

Several of these deep, mutual 'friendships across difference' have already been touched on in this chapter. It is one thing to be different from one another, but when one partner in a relationship changes, especially through illness, there is a further journey in the relationship, as anyone who has accompanied a family or community member through Alzheimer's disease or other mental illness can testify. Anthony Kramers described the adjustments needed in order to remain faithful to Bertie Fowler through the final months of Bertie's life in l'Arche Edinburgh as Alzheimer's took hold:

Many people knew him, loved and occasionally struggled with him in his years of activity, as a founder member, ambassador for l'Arche, man of fun and court jester, devoted uncle. Some have only known him in the last period of diminishment, of failing strength, of pains, fears, anxieties and disturbed nights and loss of mobility, with the special moments of wakeful presence and smiling eyes. We had to ask for help. We're born in weakness – can we create a context in which we can live the weakness leading to death? Help came from a host of services and therapists. Many shared our desire to enable Bertie to stay at home, and Bertie's own response helped us all, drawing out the unexpected from others, our own qualities of compassion and tenderness, loss and challenge, love and anger. Each person in the community has been touched, and not only the community but the whole tapestry of Bertie's family and friends, church, and people from the Health and Social Services. There have been glimpses of 'covenant' in all these faces.

A Trinity of Friends – Transfiguration
A trinity of friends
Are meeting heart to heart,

To help them send a prophet to their jubilee,
By hearsay you were known,
Till glory could be shown,
Transfiguring our lives to see you face to face.

So Peter, James and John
Are taken to one side,
And made to climb the brae;
Their heart is filled with song,
Misgivings ebb away
In seeing Jesus pray.

Each mountain we ascend,
Each joy that people share
Or friend we need to grieve;
Each noust that we prepare
In song or shared prayer
Is one we're called to leave.

The passages of life
Are made through suffering,
O how we must let go;
A glimpse of covenant is not for our control,
O how we must let go.

Song from l'Arche Edinburgh

Covenant is relationship received, to develop and to grow in. A relationship in which both, or all, parties are changed. We sometimes think of a covenant as a bi-lateral negotiated agreement between equal parties, something that we do, something we sign up to. But in the story of us and God, and subsequently one another, covenants are a totally free, uni-lateral initiative from

God, to which the people, we, say 'yes' or not. In saying 'yes' we embark upon a journey with God and with one another. Our hope, joy and perseverance on that journey come from the fact that God is faithful in covenant. Father Thomas Cullinan puts this in a modern parable:

> Suppose that in Northern Ireland, or another place of long term fears, divisions, memories, scapegoats, and violence, suppose that legitimate representatives of different factions really worked through and confronted the issues, both in themselves and for the people at large, and then came into a covenant which put every person in the land into a new reality; what then would happen out in the towns and country?
>
> In Ballyalpha the people heard the news and were so full of alleluias and celebrations that it had happened, that they did not realise the long haul involved, that they had to make the same journey in all their local social relationships, and within each family, and even within each person.
>
> The people of Ballybeta never heard the news at all, or didn't recognise what it meant. But they carried on as they had been doing, working away at the same reconciliation locally, with great endeavour, to bring about what did not exist.
>
> Ballygamma heard the news, knew its uniqueness and celebrated, but only in order to embark on the same programme locally, to 'realise' that which they now were. Along the way they failed, but each time they had a party and started again, because the reality was there ahead of them.
>
> Covenant is offered gift, not achieved endeavour.

Trusting, receiving, forgiving and being forgiven, constantly starting again, celebrating and often re-telling, re-reading the story – surely all this needs to be kept at the heart of any community, family or church? It's now nearly 40 years since Jean Vanier began living with Raphael Simi and Phillipe Seux and l'Arche began. The world is very different now and many l'Arche communities have long outgrown the founding phase. While the founding spirit is still around there is plenty of energy and idealism. We cannot rely on the same old stuff to inspire later generations, just as young people are unlikely to want to be in church for the same reasons as their parents and grandparents. So how do we remain alive and authentic? How can we receive and grow in 'covenant' relationships in a world of regulation, performance indicators, and competition for resources? In many Western countries there is thankfully far more provision for learning-disabled people than four decades ago, with considerable emphasis on choice, if not on sharing and community values. So why should l'Arche continue and what is its specific role and message?

When 300 people from all the communities of l'Arche around the world gathered at Swanwick in Derbyshire in May 2002 (see chapter 3) it was to celebrate the story so far and to look ahead, asking 'what are we here for?' questions. In the process of naming our identity and mission in today's world we are all asked to look again at our founding 'myth', our personal and community stories, and to re-read them in the light of the needs and questions around us. This is an immensely hopeful and risky process of prayer and discernment, of listening to what we've been given through our relationships, and where we need such relationships today. Relationships of mutuality and service that 'construct each other's humanity', as Rowan Williams put it.

It is easy to assume that we know what we are in l'Arche for. I have worked for many years in the weaving workshop of l'Arche Liverpool and reckon that I have a pretty clear idea of the value of work in giving dignity and a sense of worth. Robert

McWilliam has worked there longer than I have. Robert is a small, sometimes fearful man who has Down's Syndrome. Everything he does is towards relationship. One day there were five of us working in the room and since Robert is a competent weaver I began to pay more attention to the loom that a less experienced assistant was struggling to thread up with Ian. After a bit Robert called out 'Talk to me!' I, but not Robert, am always in danger of becoming too absorbed by function, too busy, like Martha, to be ready for the 'one thing needed' (Luke 10). It's right that we have to conform to high standards of care and training today but in this climate of regulation we need also to be careful not to get too busy to listen, to celebrate, to waste time together.

I am still in touch with a family that I got to know in Central America many years ago. They are certainly among the dispossessed. Life in such countries is more and more difficult as international debt and corruption bleed their economies and disasters such as Hurricane Mitch, which tore through Honduras and Nicaragua in 1998, wreak further devastation. But what Adriana and her family value more than anything I can do, is our friendship. A friendship that leaves me powerless and vulnerable too when the hurricane strikes, or a family member is killed crossing a border to find work. It's taken me 30 years to learn that from Adriana and from Robert, Ian and so many others whose stories have been touched on here. Of course we must continue to struggle for justice, for changes in the structures of power that divide and destroy in our world. But those changes can only take place truthfully when we recognise the source of our relationships, mutual relationships that we discover only in letting go of our own terms and conditions.

In a recent lecture with members of an aid agency Dominican priest Timothy Radcliffe spelt this out vividly:

God's creation of humanity is not ultimately the production of individuals. God brings to birth a community in which we can all say 'we' and so flourish humanly. This is the Kingdom. It is only when we can say 'we' that we shall understand what it means for any of us to say 'I am' . . . Apart from each other we are incomplete.

This new communion for which we labour is defined by more than mere geographical extension. It is a belonging together that is usually called 'solidarity' . . . 'Solidarity' is a word whose roots lie in early nineteenth-century France. It meant the solidarity of the French against such enemies as the English. We Christians aspire to an unimaginable solidarity that is not against anyone. It is not based on exclusion, of an 'us' against 'them' . . . The Kingdom is solidarity without exclusion, offering us an identity beyond our present understanding. Until the Kingdom, we are incomplete people. It is not only the poor, the powerless and the voiceless who lack full identity. We do too, until we are one with them . . . It is only in the 'we' of the Kingdom that we shall each know what it means to say 'I am'.[10]

Solidarity, unity, becoming one, is a challenge, an imperative and a life long work. But before all that it is an invitation, an invitation to become who we are, to be ourselves. Costly but hope filled, as Thérèse Vanier's prayer expresses:

> May oppressed people and those who oppress them, free each other
> May those who are handicapped, and those who think they are not, help each other
> May those who need someone to listen touch the hearts of those who are too busy

May the homeless bring joy to those who open their doors
    reluctantly

May the lonely heal those who think they are self sufficient

May the poor melt the hearts of the rich

May seekers for truth give life to those who are satisfied that
    they have found it

May the dying who do not wish to die be comforted by those
    who find it hard to live

May the unloved be allowed to unlock the hearts of those who
    cannot love

May prisoners find true freedom and liberate others from fear

May those who sleep on the streets share their gentleness with
    those who cannot understand them

May the hungry tear the veil from the eyes of those who do
    not hunger after justice

May those who live without hope cleanse the hearts of their
    brothers and sisters who are afraid to live

May the weak confound the strong and save them

May violence be overcome by compassion

May violence be absorbed by men and women of peace

May violence succumb to those who are totally vulnerable

That we may be healed
Amen.[11]

Further Information

To know more about l'Arche communities in Britain, please contact:
l'Arche UK Secretariat, 10 Briggate, Silsden, Keighley, West Yorkshire BD20 9JT.
Tel: 01535 656186; Fax: 01535 656426; E-mail: info@larche.org.uk
or visit the website www.larche.org.uk

For l'Arche International, write to:
10 rue Fenoux, 75015 PARIS, France.
Tel: 00 33 1 68 08 00; E-mail: international@larche.org
or visit the website www.larche.org

For information about Faith and Light communities, please contact:
Aslaug Espe, Skogfaret 10, 1430 As, Norway
Tel: 00 476 494 2641; Fax: 00 476 496 3861; E-mail: aslaugespe@c2i.net

Music for the songs quoted from the Da Noust collection of L'Arche Edinburgh
can be obtained by writing to:
L'Arche, 132 Constitution Street, Edinburgh EH6 6AJ.

Further Reading

International Council of l'Arche, *Ecumenism in l'Arche* (2 vols) (1994)*

Tim Kearney (ed), *A Prophetic Cry* (Veritas, 2000)

Henri J. M. Nouwen, *Adam: God's Beloved* (Darton, Longman and Todd, 1997)

Henri J. M. Nouwen, *Finding My Way Home: Pathways to Life and the Spirit* (Darton, Longman and Todd, 2001)

Henri J. M. Nouwen, *The Road to Daybreak* (Darton, Longman and Todd, 1989 and 1997)

Ruth Patterson, *A Further Shore* (Veritas, 2000)

Beth Porter with Susan S. M. Brown and Philip Coulter (eds), *Befriending Life: Encounters with Henri Nouwen* (Darton, Longman and Todd, 2001)

Helen Reid Thomas, *L'Arche* (Catholic Truth Society, 2002)

Thérèse Vanier, *Nick: Man of the Heart* (Gill and Macmillan, 1993)*

Thérèse Vanier, *One Bread, One Body* (Gracewing, 1997)*

Jean Vanier, *An Ark for the Poor: The Story of l'Arche* (Novalis/Geoffrey Chapman, 1995)

Jean Vanier, *Becoming Human* (Darton, Longman and Todd, 1999)

Jean Vanier, *Community and Growth* (Darton, Longman and Todd, 1989)

Jean Vanier, *The Heart of L'Arche: A Spirituality for Every Day* (Novalis/Geoffrey Chapman, 1995)

Jean Vanier, *Made for Happiness: Discovering the Meaning of Life with Aristotle* (Darton, Longman and Todd, 2001)

Jean Vanier, *Our Journey Home* (Hodder and Stoughton, 1997)

Frances Young (ed), *Encounter with Mystery* (Darton, Longman and Todd, 1997)

A full list of books, booklets and video tapes is available from l'Arche UK Secretariat.

* out of print, but obtainable from l'Arche UK Secretariat.

Notes

1. *Encounter with Mystery* edited by Frances Young (Darton, Longman and Todd, 1997), p. 5.
2. Da Noust, an Orcadian word for a boat shelter, gathers and shares some of the creative activities of l'Arche Edinburgh, including the prayers, songs and blessings from that community used in this book.
3. *One Bread, One Body* by Thérèse Vanier (Novalis/Gracewing, 1997), p. 72.
4. *Ecumenism in l'Arche* (1), International Council of l'Arche, February 1994, p. 34.
5. *Finding My Way Home* by Henri J. M. Nouwen (Darton, Longman and Todd, 2000), p. 72.
6. *One Bread, One Body*, p. 80.
7. Music to 'No longer strangers but pilgrims together' can be obtained by writing to l'Arche Beni Abbes (see Further Information for contact details).
8. *One Bread, One Body*, p. 72.
9. *On Christian Theology* by Rowan Williams (Blackwell, 2000), p. 232.
10. 'Pope Paul VI Memorial Lecture' by Timothy Radcliffe, published in *The Tablet*, 14 December 2002.
11. *One Bread, One Body*, preface.